TIRPITZ

MILITARY PROFILES

SERIES EDITOR
Dennis E. Showalter, Ph.D.
Colorado College

*Instructive summaries for general and expert
readers alike, volumes in the Military Profiles
series are essential treatments of significant and
popular military figures drawn from world history,
ancient times through the present.*

TIRPITZ

Architect of the German High Seas Fleet

Michael Epkenhans

Potomac Books, Inc.
Washington, D.C.

Library of Congress Cataloging-in-Publication Data
Epkenhans, Michael.
  Tirpitz : architect of the German high seas fleet / Michael Epkenhans.
      p. cm. — (Military profiles)
  Includes bibliographical references and index.
  ISBN 978-1-57488-444-9 (hardcover : alk. paper) — ISBN 978-1-
57488-732-7 (pbk. : alk. paper)
 1. Tirpitz, Alfred von, 1a849-1930. 2. Admirals—Germany—Biography.
3. Germany. Kriegsmarine—History—19th century 4. Germany.
Kriegsmarine—History—20th century. 5. Germany—History, Naval—
19th century. 6. Germany—History, Naval—20th century. 7. Sea-
power—Germany—History—19th century. 8. Sea-power—Germany—
History—20th century. I. Title.
  DD231.T5E65 2008
  359.0092—dc22
  [B]

                                          2008023681

Printed in the United States of America on acid-free paper that meets
the American National Standards Institute Z39-48 Standard.

Potomac Books, Inc.
22841 Quicksilver Drive
Dulles, Virginia 20166

First Edition

10 9 8 7 6 5 4 3 2 1

Contents

Preface and Acknowledgments

Grand Admiral Alfred von Tirpitz played an important role in German, politics at the turn of the twentieth century. As "father of the German Battle Fleet," he was one of the key figures responsible for both the "cold war" that led to the outbreak of World War I in July 1914 as well as the challenge to Britain's supremacy at sea and in world politics. Political defeat in 1918 did not end Tirpitz's career. Until his death in 1930, as "grey excellence" he tried to rally the political right behind himself in an attempt to change the new democratic political order established in 1918 after the collapse of the empire.

Long before he became a naval politician, Tirpitz had been a professional naval officer in the Prussian and Imperial German Navy. After active duty in Spanish waters during the Carlist revolt in the 1870s, he became a member of the newly created Torpedo Research and Development Section of the Admiralty. Here, he showed his talents and energy in fulfilling the tasks he had been assigned to. Within a few years, he and the members of his torpedo gang developed the torpedo boat into a modern, highly effective weapon.

In 1891, Tirpitz, then Chief of Staff of the Baltic Naval Station attracted the attention of the young Kaiser, Wilhelm II. The Kaiser, who was also a naval enthusiast, was deeply impressed by Tirpitz's ideas and systematic approach to naval strategy and tactics as well as naval politics.

This relationship with the Kaiser paved the way for Tirpitz's appointment to be Secretary of State for the Navy in 1897. Tirpitz seemed the only man to be energetic and unscrupulous enough to overcome the difficulties the Kaiser's naval plans had encountered before. He did not disappoint the Kaiser. Between 1898 and 1912, Tirpitz built up a powerful battle fleet.

However, when war broke out in 1914, this fleet failed to achieve its aims. The decisive battle between the High Seas Fleet and the Royal Navy never took place. In March 1916, the Emperor had lost his confidence in his most prominent naval officer and dismissed him.

This dismissal opened up new opportunities for Tirpitz. He soon became a leading member of the political right, pleading for far-reaching annexations and blocking any domestic reforms. After the war he continued fighting along this line, hoping to help Germany become an authoritarian powerful nation once again.

Tirpitz was unique among the German leaders, both in politics and in the military. Unlike many contemporaries, he had not only great visions, but also a strong will to realize his aims. His propaganda campaigns illustrate that he had a modern approach to solving political, military, and bureaucratic problems in a mass society. Like many great men, however, he was unwilling to compromise about important questions of foreign policy or naval strategy, always preferring an "all or nothing" strategy. That is why he failed before and during the war.

Many individuals have helped to finish this manuscript. My friends from the German Navy—Captains FN Dr. Werner Rahn and Dr. Jörg Duppler, Commanders Dr. Jörg Hillman and Dr. Frank Nägler, Colonel Dr. Hans Ehlert, and Lieutentant Colonel Dr. Gerhard Gross of the German Army—provided advice on strategic and technical matters. I also have to thank Professors Volker R. Berghahn, Wilhelm Deist (+) and Holger Herwig who paved the way for me and who encouraged me to write this book as well as Professor Patrick J. Kelly, who is working on a biography on Tirpitz himself and whom I got to know at a rather late stage of writing this book. Instead of being competitors, he and I freely exchanged our views and documents. My colleagues and students at Hamburg University were always willing to discuss the problems of a modern biography. I am also deeply indebted to Jennifer Waldrop, Katie Freemann, and all the other helping hands from Books International for their almost endless patience and for their efforts to polish the manuscript.

Most important of all was the support of my wife and my children, Daniel and Anne, who were always tolerant enough to share their lives with Tirpitz. The book is dedicated to my son Daniel, who has shared my interest in the navy and its history since he was a young boy and has been an excellent comrade in all these years.

Chronology

1849, March 19	Alfred von Tirpitz is born in Küstrin
1865, April 24	Enters Prussian Navy
1868–1869	Attends Naval School at Kiel
1869, September 22	Promoted to Second Lieutenant
1872, May 22	Promoted to First Lieutenant
1874–1876	Attends Naval Academy at Kiel
1875, November 18	Promoted to Lieutenant Commander
1877–1886	Joins Torpedo Research and Development Section of the Admiralty
1881, September 17	Promoted to Commander
1886–1889	Becomes Inspector of Torpedo Boat Division
1888, November 24	Promoted to Captain
1889, April 29	Takes command of *Preußen*
1890, May 2	Takes command of *Württemberg*
1890, September 27	Becomes Chief of Staff of the Baltic Naval Station
1895–1896	Becomes Chief of Staff of the High Command
1895, May 13	Promoted to Rear Admiral
1896, June 15	Takes command of the East Asian Cruiser Squadron
1897, June 15	Becomes Secretary of State for the Imperial Navy Office
1899, December 5	Promoted to Vice Admiral
1900, January 1	Is enobled
1903, November 14	Promoted to Admiral

1911, January 27	Promoted to Grand Admiral
1916, March 16	Is dismissed
1924–1928	Becomes a member of the *Reichstag* for the Deutsch-Nationale Volkspartei
1930, March 6	Dies in Ebenhausen

Young Tirpitz

Alfred Peter Friedrich Tirpitz was born on March 19, 1849, in Küstrin on the Oder River, today a part of Poland. He grew up in Frankfurt-on-the-Oder, where his father had been appointed a judge at the local law court.

It is very likely that the Tirpitz family had been part of the Silesian nobility in the sixteenth, seventeenth, and eighteenth centuries. However, they lost their fortune during the Seven Years' War and gave up their title before his birth. Impoverished Tirpitz's ancestors had left Silesia and settled down in the Prussian province of Brandenburg.[1] His great-grandfather had joined the Prussian Army to become staff-trumpeter of a famous dragoon regiment and been a salt-trader in his later years. Tirpitz's grandfather had studied law to become a judge, a profession his father also found attractive.

Since the early 1800s, the Tirpitz family belonged to the upper-bourgeois classes. Traditional Prussian values, such as a strong feeling of doing one's duty for the king and the nation, love of the fatherland, and parsimony were of great importance in family life. Prussia's fall and rise again during the Napoleonic Wars had a deep impact upon Tirpitz's father. The heroes of the War of Liberation in 1814–15, such as Generals Scharnhorst and Gneisenau as well as Prussia's most important philosophers at the turn of the century, Immanuel Kant and Johann Gottlieb Fichte, had deeply influenced him. In Berlin, Tirpitz's father had attended the same school as Otto von Bismarck, Germany's "Iron Chancellor." Education there seems to have been so liberal that even Bismarck later claimed that he was a convinced republican when he left school in 1832.

Whether Tirpitz's father was also a republican is unknown, although he seems to have shared liberal ideas to some extent. However, he had always been loyal to the Prussian king. In 1848–49, as an officer of the Prussian Army Reserve, the *Landwehr*, he had even taken part in crushing Polish uprisings in Prussia's eastern provinces.

Young Tirpitz grew up in this environment. According to a biographical sketch of his father's life, written by Tirpitz's eldest son during the latter's internment in the Netherlands in 1918, Tirpitz fully internalized his father's attitudes and virtues.[2] "If man does not have the courage to do something, he must *want* to have it," became one of the most important mottoes of his life.

The impact of Prussian virtues upon his life was further enhanced on long, daily walks, during which Tirpitz's father introduced his son to Prussian history. These stories helped to shape Tirpitz according to the example of Scharnhorst and Clausewitz. Prussia's greatest king, Frederick II, however, was Tirpitz's most important idol for the rest of his life. His son remembers how he read Carlyle's biography on "Frederick the Great" multiple times in search of advice.

Tirpitz's mother, whose ancestors were of French origins, was deeply religious, warm-hearted, and always ready to help. She was also interested in literature. She often organized amateur theater plays for her sons and their friends at home. However, she failed to pass her inclinations down to Alfred, her third son.

At home, Alfred "was the most loveable, most attentive son," his parents could wish. When he went out into the streets, however, "he was a wild, daring child," always eager to fight.[3] At school, Tirpitz was a mediocre student. Instead of a *Gymnasium*, his father had sent his three sons to a *Realschule,* thus hoping to improve their knowledge of the exact sciences. Teaching there was, as Tirpitz claimed in his memoirs, inefficient.[4] "At Christmas 1864 my certificate was 'Moderate,'" he remembered. Accordingly, he wanted to leave school as soon as possible. The Prussian Navy offered a way out of this dilemma. Though he had no idea of what it meant to become a naval officer and take up such a life, he asked his parents for permission to leave school for the navy. They received this idea "in complete silence" when confronted the first time, but his father approved of it. Surprised by the decision, Alfred promised to pass the entrance examination at the Naval Cadet's Institute in Berlin in return. "I kept my word," he proudly remembered almost sixty years later, and in 1865, "passed, to everybody's surprise, fifth on the list, and became a sailor."[5]

An Able and Ambitious Naval Officer

On April 24, 1865, only a few weeks after his sixteenth birthday, Tirpitz was appointed naval cadet in the Prussian Navy. On May 15, he reported for duty at Kiel. Tirpitz's time at school was over at last. Looking back almost sixty years later, Tirpitz was surprised his entry into the navy was the beginning of a great career.

Though Prussia had embarked on an offensive foreign policy aiming at improving its position both within the German Confederation, the *Deutsche Bund*, and among the European powers, it was questionable whether the Prussian Navy would play a more important role in the future.

During the revolution of 1848, the Danish blockade of the German North Sea and Baltic coasts aroused great enthusiasm for the navy both in liberal circles and in Prussia. To meet the Danish challenge, the Diet of Frankfurt appointed Prince Adalbert, the cousin of the King of Prussia, to a position similar to a minister of the navy. Prince Adalbert built up the first *Reichsmarine* in German history by buying vessels abroad. These efforts contrasted with Prussia's endeavors to develop its own navy, highlighting the peculiarities of German history in the nineteenth century. In September 1848, a royal decree elevated the small

Prussian naval force from the status of a small *Küstenflottille* to a proper navy. In March 1849, when the decline of the Diet of Frankfurt was obvious, another royal decree appointed Prince Adalbert chief of the Naval High Command, the *Oberkommando der Marine*.

The suppression of the revolutionary movement by Prussian troops and the end of the conflict with Denmark in 1850 had far-reaching consequences for the *Reichsmarine* and the Prussian Navy. While the ships of the former were eventually sold at an official auction in 1852, the development of the latter was soon slowed down. Nevertheless, Prince Adalbert did his best to defend the navy against demands to dissolve it and to assign all naval officers to the Army Corps of Engineers. In 1853, the navy's administration was separated from the army and placed under the Royal Prussian Admiralty, the *Königliche Preußische Admiralität*. In 1854, Prince Adalbert was promoted to the rank of Admiral of the Prussian Coast, *Admiral der Preußischen Küste*. In 1859, a Prussian naval squadron consisting of four vessels left for the Far East to establish political and commercial relations with Japan, China, and Siam, and also to emphasize the importance of sea power and world politics. However, for the foreseeable future, Prussia's status among the powers would depend on its army, not its navy.

In 1862 and 1865, the Prussian Minister of War, General Albrecht von Roon, submitted new building programs to the Prussian Parliament, the *Abgeordnetenhaus,* which emancipated the navy from the army. Roon's twelve-year program was modest in scope, aspiring only to second-class naval strength. He proposed the construction of new naval bases at Wilhelmshaven on the North Sea and on the island of Rugen in the Baltic as well as the build-up of a fleet composed of ten armored frigates, ten larger coastal-defense units, and fourteen ships for the protection and disruption of trade. In the future, the Prussian Navy would have an offensive capability to attack enemy shipping and hostile fleets, coasts, and harbors. However, Roon's demand for the allocation of money in 1862 highlighted the priority of the army over the navy. Whereas the former was to receive 38.5 million talers, the navy's budget amounted to 2.3 million.[1] Considering the dangers on Prussia's land fronts, it was questionable whether the Prussian Navy would increase its budget.

The navy Roon wanted to build was not the navy Tirpitz entered. In 1865, the Prussian Navy consisted only of a small number of varying vessels: a screw-propelled force of three corvettes, one yacht, and twenty-one gunboats, supplemented by two paddle steamers. Many of these vessels were old, conveying "an atmosphere of the Middle Ages" as Tirpitz described when he explained the need of avoiding a fight with superior Austrian forces.[2] However, deficiencies in material and size were not the only problems of the Prussian Navy.

The fact that the navy, unlike the army, had no tradition of a glorious past was also responsible for the fact that its reputation was poor and its attraction to new recruits only slight. Prussian conservatives distrusted the idea of a fleet. "It was not considered to be in keeping with the Prussian tradition, it competed in some degree with the army, it seemed too closely related with industry and commerce in view of the agricultural distress of that time and the great economic conflicts of the parties."[3]

The sinking of the corvette LSMS *Amazone* in a storm off the Dutch coast in 1861 with all naval cadets on board reduced the number of qualified officers for many years to come. Moreover, this event also had a great impact on the attraction of the navy in general. In 1865, Tirpitz was one of only ten applicants.

The lack of interest in the navy both by traditional Prussian conservatives and the younger generation corresponded with the "confusion in our Naval Officer's Corps," which numbered only 120 officers in those days.[4] Roon had asked to increase it to two hundred naval officers, *Seeoffiziere*, two hundred warrant officers, *Deckoffiziere*, and 5,400 enlisted men, but it would take time to find and train them. In the meantime, due to the lack of experienced officers, parts of the naval officers' corps came from cavalry regiments. Some had been trained in the German or Danish navies; others came from Britain, the United States, and Holland, or had served in the merchant navy. It was not until after 1870 that the navy began to remove some of these "remarkable characters," as Tirpitz called them. But many of those who remained went their own way or became cranks; at the best they were self-taught. Tirpitz wrote, "My year, however, was favored: we had an excellent staff, to whom I look back with gratitude."[5]

The Prussian Navy took cadets who were generally between fourteen and seventeen years old, of "good origin and upbringing, a healthy body, and had an unspoiled character open to all noble impressions."[6] The cadets took an exam before entering the navy. Those who passed it successfully boarded a training ship for a cruise, which, apart from providing practical nautical experience, tested their physical and intellectual capacities. Returning home cadets had to take a midshipmen's exam, the *Seekadettenprüfung*, which evaluated proficiency in gunnery, navigation, and seamanship. Successful midshipmen then again left for a two-year training cruise to the South Atlantic or to East Asia before entering the Naval School, the *Marineschule*, at Kiel to pass their final exams and receive their commissions as first lieutenants and to swear an oath of duty and honor to the Prussian king.[7]

The sources about Tirpitz's early years in the navy are scarce. Some of his official logbooks have survived. However, since he had to keep them according to a fixed scheme, they hardly contain any information about events, his personal feelings, or the officers on board and his fellow cadets. Instead, they only give a detailed account of daily routine on board like "sabre-exercise," "watch-times," "temperatures," or "wind and sea states."[8] Whether he also kept a private logbook is unknown. However, letters he wrote to his parents and brother from his first training cruise give fairly good descriptions of his life on board or on land stations and about his opinion about naval as well as political affairs.[9]

According to these letters he seems to have enjoyed his new life. He was anticipating getting "out of Europe," he wrote on June 27, 1865, after he had been told that SM Training Ship *Niobe* would leave for the West Indies in the fall.[10] On September 26, Tirpitz finally left for Plymouth, then for a long training cruise into the Atlantic Ocean calling at Tenerife, the Cape Verde islands, the Caribbean islands, and Spain and Portugal to return home in spring 1866.

The crew consisted of twenty-three cadets, some of them coming from the merchant navy. They were all of the same class, for only affluent families could afford sending their sons to the navy. Among the members of the crew were three future admirals: Otto von Diederichs, future commander of the Cruiser Squadron, which occupied Kiautchou in 1897 and Chief of the Admiral Staff, the *Admiralstab*, in 1899,

Wilhelm Büchsel, Chief of the *Admiralstab* between 1902 and 1905, and Iwan Oldekop. Though some of them, like Büchsel, were members of Tirpitz's infamous "torpedo-gang," about which we will hear later on, all of them became his rivals.

Becoming a naval officer required good health, personal fitness, and a strong will, for daily life on sailing vessels was difficult. On its passage to the West Indies the *Niobe* had to weather heavy storms that caused enormous damage to the ship. Under hazardous conditions, the cadets had to join the crew to repair the ship.[11] Weeks later, a fire broke out, extinguished only minutes before the flames reached the powder magazine. Only a few days later, the ship was again severely damaged in a storm, and all cadets and the crew made the necessary repairs in a life-and-death struggle.

While the *Niobe* sailed westwards, training continued: sail drill and gunnery practice, small arms exercises and training in amphibious operations during short land trips were occasionally interrupted by opportunities for recreation or short holidays. The discipline on board was harsh. Nevertheless, Tirpitz never complained, nor did he criticize *Niobe*'s captain, Captain Batsch, "a man with a great reputation in the Atlantic Ocean and an excellent sailor."[12] Instead, he later wrote: "Duty centred in the main in learning how to handle rigging. The art of navigation as it evolved through the centuries required long training for officers and ratings. As was usual in the days of the sailing ships, we had various adventures [...], which made us understand the days of Marryat and Nelson as though we had lived in them ourselves."[13]

Returning to Kiel in May 1866, Tirpitz and his fellow cadets had to pass their final exams, their *Seekadettenprüfung*. These exams evaluated his knowledge of gunnery, navigation, and seamanship. Tirpitz belonged to the minority who received "royal commendation" for their high scores.[14] On June 24, 1866, he was appointed sea cadet.

When Tirpitz passed his exam, Prussia and Austria were at war and all cadets were ordered to report for duty. Tirpitz went on board SMS *Gazelle*, a corvette, without seeing any action apart from lying in Kiel harbor with loaded guns to guard the army's advance into the Duchy of Holstein and the retreat of the Austrians under the tunes of a Prussian band.[15] The only significant event for him was that he was almost drowned when he tried to save the life of another sailor who had fallen over board.[16]

On August 1, 1866, after the war with Austria was over, Tirpitz began midshipman training aboard the SMS *Musquito*. This time, they left Kiel for a cruise to the Mediterranean, calling at Monte Carlo, Nice, Marseilles, and Genoa. Back at Kiel in June 1867, he was transferred to SMS *Gefion* for almost two months before he had to report for duty on SMS *Thetis* for another long cruise.

The victory over Austria and the founding of the North German Confederation, which united all states north of the River Main under Prussian leadership, had a deep impact on the role of its navy. In October 1867, General von Roon presented a new plan to parliament, the *Reichstag,* demanding the construction of sixteen armored ships, twenty corvettes, eight dispatch boats, three transport ships, twenty-two steam-driven gunboats, two artillery training ships, and five school ships. Though the offensive capability of this force was played down, the navy of the North German Confederation would indeed be a formidable force in the near future, for the Naval Ministry succeeded to commission the construction of five armored ships in 1869–1871.[17]

Tirpitz knew that an important change had taken place: "Our reputation had risen considerably in 1866. Once before we had felt humiliated at the way we had been looked upon in Cadiz when the Spanish officer kept us waiting for the quayside inspection. But in Marseilles in 1867 the people came rushing on board to see the Prussians. In Nice needle-guns were exhibited in the fair-booth."[18]

Returning home from his training cruises in 1868, Tirpitz proceeded to the final step of officer training and reported to the Navy School, the *Marineschule,* at Kiel. The curriculum of the Navy School contained courses in mathematics, natural science, French and English, navigation, gunnery, military and naval tactics, ship design, steam engineering, and naval protocol as well as fencing, gymnastics and swimming. Tirpitz and his fellow cadets had to work very hard. In November he wrote that five of his fellow classmater already had been ordered to leave in his first weeks. In February 1869, he told his parents "my life here is not very pleasant in general. […] The lectures are proceeding at such a tearing pace that it is difficult to follow them completely."[19] In spite of the strain he suffered, Tirpitz passed his exam successfully and was appointed sub-lieutenant, *Unterleutnant zur See*, on September 22, 1869.

Having received his commission and having committed himself to the service of the crown "with honor and duty,"[20] Tirpitz had to proceed to the Artillery Test Commission, the *Artillerieprüfungskommission*, at Berlin to attend a course on gunnery. On May 1, 1870 he was ordered to report for duty on SMS *König Wilhelm*, an armored frigate that was the flagship of the navy's sortie force, the *Ausfallflotte*. In spring, four ships of the squadron were to sail for the Azores for training purposes.

Tirpitz later described this cruise as an interesting experience in many ways. First, though SMS *König Wilhelm* was an armored frigate, training was "still influenced by the customs of the sailing ships: we even tried to sail on this voyage, but the hulks refused to move."[21] Second, for lack of dockyard facilities as well as experience with iron-hulled vessels, the ships were in bad condition, their hulls had not been cleaned since they had been commissioned years before. SMS *König Wilhelm* had over sixty tons of mussels on her bottom, reducing her speed from sixteen to ten knots. Third, the engine of the ship broke down in the Channel, compelling the crew to run into Plymouth for a lengthy period of repair.

However, on July 16, 1870, SMS *König Wilhelm* and the other ships of the squadron were ordered back to Wilhelmshaven when France declared war against Prussia. Though it was a land war, two French squadrons soon operated in the North Sea and in the Baltic blockading the German coasts.

When news had reached the SMS *König Wilhelm* that war with France was imminent and that a French squadron was cruising in the Channel, Tirpitz hoped that his squadron would attack it despite lack of coal and ammunition. "The quality of our ships and of our guns would have made up for our inferiority in numbers,"[22] he wrote to his parents, thus using an argument he would refer to when justifying the build-up of an inferior battle-fleet at the turn of century. To Tirpitz's disappointment and dismay, the fleet lay at anchor in Wilhelmshaven to go into action only if Hamburg or any other place on the North Sea coast was attacked. The fleet only left twice to watch the French squadron cruising in the North Sea.[23]

In hindsight, Tirpitz admitted that Admiral Jachmann's decision to remain on the defensive had been correct: "In view of the lack of any possibility of refitting we had to risk the loss of our whole fleet, without gaining any advantage."[24]

Nevertheless, in 1870, the fact that the army was victorious in paving the way for unification while the fleet stayed in its harbors "lay heavily on the navy." Tirpitz spent months "on the projecting ram of the *König Wilhelm*, keeping a look-out for our mines, although this would have been just as useless for catching loose mines in the misty autumn weather as the floating wooden barricade attached to the bowsprit of the ship."[25]

In December, due to heavy weather, the ships had to enter Wilhelmshaven harbor, which was still under construction. For the crews of the vessels, this was no relief. Instead, "partly in order to maintain discipline, and partly because it was thought that the navy ought to be tackled in a more military manner and brought up to a more soldierly standard, a tremendous amount of infantry drill was carried out in the winter months."[26]

Despite the strain he suffered, Tirpitz had enough time to reflect upon politics in general as well as the future of the navy in particular. After the outbreak of war, he watched the nationalistic tide that was sweeping Germany as well as the events on the battlefields with great enthusiasm. "Reading the news about the national temper is really elevating,"[27] he wrote on July 18, 1870. On January 23, 1871, he wrote to his parents: "If a continuation of the war would not mean that we would have to deplore greater losses of men, it could only be favourable for us, if the French would continue to work with us to ruin themselves. The more this country will be ruined, the less will we have to be afraid of this enemy in the future."[28] In Bismarck's opinion, only by weakening France strategically and militarily could a French war of revenge be postponed and peace in Europe secured.

Moreover, Tirpitz also began to deal with naval strategy as well as naval politics in great detail considering he was only a twenty-two-year old sub-lieutenant.[29] In a famous letter to his father he dealt extensively with three questions raised by an anonymous naval officer in an article published by a popular journal, the *Gartenlaube*: First, do we in fact need a navy? Second, what kinds of vessels are most useful for our navy? Third, where should these vessels be built?[30] In this letter, Tirpitz argued that only a battle fleet, which operated offensively, could protect Germany's sea-interests.

With the war ending in May, he was appointed first officer on a gunboat, the SMS *Blitz*. "This outpost was left on the frontier, forgotten; we had light river- and harbour-police duties; in general however, we were only for show and enjoyed Hamburg's friendship until Stosch found out in the autumn of 1872 that we were kicking our heels there, and cancelled the command."[31] This was an honest description of his time on *Blitz* following his letters to his parents.[32] Leaving SMS *Blitz* in September 1872, Tirpitz became an officer of the watch on the armored frigate SMS *Friedrich Carl* and soon left for a long cruise into the Atlantic Ocean and the West Indies. Tirpitz enjoyed this long time at sea as well as the experience of seeing the world: "Salem Aleykum. Many greetings from your son from the country of the Emperor of Fez and of Morocco. There can be no greater cultural difference anywhere in the world than the one you find crossing the Strait of Gibraltar to this place [Tangiers],"[33] he wrote to his parents in January 1873. Returning to Kiel in April 1874, Tirpitz joined the Naval Academy, the *Marineakademie* for a two-year course.

The fact that Tirpitz's application had been accepted was indeed proof that he was an able and ambitious young naval officer. Applicants had to submit a résumé and three essays from a list of topics including naval history, navigation, gunnery, steam engineering, and naval architecture.[34] Tirpitz passed these tests and was recommended for acceptance in 1874, but despite his abilities and ambitions, he had not always been easy to deal with. According to the judgment of the commander of SMS *Friedrich Carl,* Captain Reinhold von Werner, "he would be an excellent officer, if he had more discipline. [...] He will be able to be appointed to higher positions only if he has proven continually that he is willing to obey orders."[35]

Some of his biographers claim that this was unjust, for Tirpitz had only defended either subordinates or fellow officers against their superiors. That as it may, Tirpitz, who had been appointed lieutenant commander, *Kapitänleutnant*, on November 18, 1875, slowly worked his way up in the navy.

A Man of New Ideas

On January 1, 1877, after two years at sea on board the armored cruiser TSMS *Kronprinz*, Tirpitz became a member of the Torpedo Research and Development Section of the Admiralty in Berlin. This appointment was a routine placement, but it became an important step in Tirpitz's future career. It was here that he came into close contact with the Chief of the Admiralty, Admiral Albrecht von Stosch and his successor, Admiral Leo von Caprivi, two highly competent generals. General Stosch dedicated himself to the task of building up a navy systematically. In 1873, a first fleet development plan, *Flottengründungsplan*, was passed by the *Reichstag*, which aimed at building up a navy consisting of six armored frigates, eighteen corvettes, and six gunboats. There were to be two overseas stations, an overseas squadron, and a substantial reserve as well.

Tirpitz praised Stosch for these actions later and remained in contact with him for the rest of his life. "Stosch took up again the broken thread of the Hansa; he was the first to feel his way towards a future for Germany overseas. He did a great deal also to breathe a fighting spirit into the navy. Mistakes were made, but in those days we were not dealing in trifles; a grave earnestness characterized our work,"[1]

Tirpitz was willing to seize the great opportunities he was offered when he became a member of the torpedo-section of the Admiralty. This section had been set up to examine the torpedo—a revolution in naval warfare. Invented by an English engineer, the torpedo could sink a naval vessel by damaging its hull under water. Its use, Tirpitz remembered, still constituted "a greater danger to the man who launched it than to his enemy."[2] Stosch, who had ordered large numbers of torpedoes in Fiume, the place of production in Austria, had asked for special reports dealing with the problems of this new weapon. Stosch regarded Tirpitz's report as "exemplary."[3] Based on his study of the torpedo in Fiume, Tirpitz gave an impressive analysis of the role of this new weapon in naval warfare and of the importance of a navy in war in general. In the years to follow, he tested the new weapon and built up the most efficient torpedo boat division then in existence.[4] Building up the navy's torpedo arm was no "soft job,"[5] as he later recalled. But he enjoyed a position of independence, which challenged his skills as a naval officer and offered opportunities to dwell upon principles of naval tactics and strategy. As captain of the tender *Zieten*, he soon displayed the qualities, that would prove decisive in his future career. Contrary to many of the old sea-dogs from the age of sail, he had realized that technology was about to fundamentally change the nature of naval warfare and that the adoption of new technology required "technical accuracy" as well as new ideas of how to use it in battle successfully. Tirpitz soon proved that he was an able officer and a man of new ideas. Although the "difficult and painfully exact task was less congenial,"[6] it trained him in method. In endless trials he tested and improved the new weapon. He put up plans for the establishment of a state torpedo shop and he also made first contacts with shipbuilding firms. Moreover, he realized that success was the result of teamwork. He assembled a group of men around him who shared his ideas and who were dedicated to the solution of the problems they were facing. The members of this "Torpedo Gang" later became his most important supporters in the build-up of the German battle fleet.

In his answer to Caprivi's "Twelve tactical questions" of 1888, Tirpitz, who had been appointed Director of the Torpedo Inspection in 1886, demonstrated that he had a clear idea of the role of torpedo boats in naval warfare. In his covering letter he demanded a "clarifying consensus" about tactical questions in the officer corps. "I personally believe, although it is not a conclusive belief, that such a consensus is achievable in peacetime and this possibility would substantially improve our chances in case of war because the qualities necessary to do this—system, perseverance and a military vision—can be found in a not insignificant degree in our national character."[7] It was this attitude that laid the foundations of his success in the 1890s.

In the 1870s and 1880s the navy didn't have a clear idea of its strategic purpose or tactics. Whereas Stosch had a definite shipbuilding program, Caprivi's "political prejudices crippled shipbuilding."[8] Technological progress was so fast and had revolutionized naval warfare in such a short time that all navies had difficulties in solving the problems they were now facing. Accordingly, the Imperial Navy did in fact live "from hand-to-mouth," because "the views that prevailed in the naval officers' corps itself were far too vague to allow a definite shipbuilding policy to crystallize."[9]

For the time being Tirpitz had no chance of developing the system he had demanded in his letter to Caprivi. In 1888, Prince Wilhelm ascended to the throne. This event would prove to have a decisive impact on the development of the navy. Wilhelm II, the Kaiser, reorganized the navy and a real admiral, Count Alexander Monts, was appointed Chief of the Admiralty.

To Tirpitz's dismay Monts regarded his torpedo-flotilla as "mere show." As a result he asked for a new command at sea. On April 29, 1889, Tirpitz took over command of the armored cruiser SMS *Preußen* and left Germany for a long cruise into the Mediterranean.

Coming from the middle class and lacking any connections in government circles or the naval hierarchy, Tirpitz had made an astonishing career in the Imperial Navy. In November 1888, at the age of thirty-nine, he had been appointed captain; it took members of the army much longer to reach the equivalent rank of a colonel. "Tirpitz was from the beginning an unusual sea officer. In the breadth of his interest for technical, political, and 'philosophical' problems, and in his piercing and cool intellect he seems to have far surpassed his comrades. [...] Not the least of his many noteworthy characteristics was his surpassed sense for the systematic, and the tenacity with which he pursued his goal, once he recognized it."[10]

In 1884 Tirpitz married Maria, born Lipke. His wife, who was eleven years younger than he, also belonged to the middle class. Her father was an attorney with close relations to members of Prussia's Liberal Party. In the 1880s he was a member of both the *Reichstag* as well as the Diet of Prussia.

According to the available evidence this marriage seems to have been a happy one. They had four children—two sons and two daughters. Apart from their younger son, his other children accompanied his career at different stages of his life. Tirpitz always exchanged his views with them freely hoping to thus provide them with guiding principles for their lives.[11]

They spent holidays together either in the Black Forest or in a romantic summerhouse on the Italian island of Sardinia. Tirpitz's elder son Wolfgang joined the navy and nearly died during the Battle of Heligoland in August 1914, but was saved by a British torpedo boat. His daughter Margot eventually became his secretary. His daughter Ilse, who also supported her father, married Ulrich von Hassell in 1911.

The 1870s and 1880s were also important for the formation of Tirpitz's mind. Since his early childhood, Tirpitz had been interested in history and always found time to read and attend lectures on history at the University of Berlin. Most important were the lectures of Heinrich von Treitschke, a liberal historian who had turned conservative in the 1870s. Treitschke regarded a strong and powerful nation-state as the ultimate aim of Germany's policy after unification and became convinced that Great Britain had tried to prevent the rise of a potentially new rival. This view had a great impact on Tirpitz and his generation.

The development of this mental framework went hand in hand with the development of an ideology of sea power. In this respect the writings of Captain USN Alfred T. Mahan played an important role. In his books, Mahan argued that only battle fleets could achieve decisive victories at sea, which were the prerequisites of command at sea and of real sea power. On the other hand, his description of the history of naval warfare in the seventeenth and eighteenth centuries and its results conveyed a message that many of his readers found convincing. Sea power, it seemed, had a decisive impact on the rise or—if lacking—the fall of nations. Only the powers that reached out across "the great thorough-fares of the world's traffic" could survive. Tirpitz transformed this idea into an ideology that encompassed national elements of culture, poli-tics, economics, military, and even race, which influenced German na-val policy for almost half a century.

In order to implement this strategy and to establish Germany as a true sea power in the coming century, the Kaiser's naval passion and his decision to change the international situation by embarking on a new offensive course was a stroke of luck for Tirpitz as he implemented his strategy to establish Germany as a true sea power. The young Kaiser wanted to follow the example of the British Empire. While the latter had dominated the world in the eighteenth and nineteenth centuries, Germany was to take its place in the twentieth century. Unfortunately, from his point of view, he still lacked the means which would enable him "to speak a different language" in the future.[12]

In the Kaiser's eyes more ships were the best and only solution to this problem. He was convinced of the relationship between naval power and world power, which was the prerequisite of national prestige, eco-nomic wealth and social stability. The Sino-Japanese War of 1894–95 and the impending collapse of the Chinese Empire and its ensuing divi-sion among the great powers confirmed this conviction and became a new spur to his ambitions. In two lengthy speeches before members of the *Reichstag* and five hundred officers in the Prussian Royal Military Academy, he eventually developed his idea of a new energetic foreign policy based on a powerful navy: "Only he who dominates the sea can effectively reach his enemy and maintain, undisturbed by him, the free-dom of military operations."[13]

However, it took the Kaiser many years to enlarge the navy. In 1889, he had been successful only in convincing the *Reichstag* to approve the construction of four more battleships. In the early 1890s, the *Reichstag* had become obstinate for the Imperial government could not describe the political aims these vessels were supposed to help achieve, nor could it put forward a coherent strategic maritime concept and a convincing building program. The Kaiser's ideas to enlarge the navy were denounced as nothing but limitless fleet plans.

In addition to lacking a clear political vision, the Kaiser also failed to put forth a consistent building plan and a strategic concept for the military use of the additional vessels he demanded from the *Reichstag*. Due to technical developments the building policy of all naval powers had undergone a serious crisis in the 1870s and 1880s. Five great mid-nineteenth century revolutions in naval technology—the introduction of steam, the screw propeller, shell guns, rifled ordnance, and armor—had fundamentally changed the parameters of naval power and naval strategy. Contrary to the Nelsonian era, in which wooden battleships rigged with sails had been both the backbone of fleets and the guarantor of naval supremacy, a "new—mainly French—school," the so-called *jeune ecole*, maintained that their time was over. Even weaker naval powers now seemed capable of successfully challenging Great Britain, by adopting a *guerre de course* strategy which mainly relied on fast cruisers and highly sophisticated torpedo boats.

Tirpitz did not believe in this strategy. In his report to Stosch on the torpedo question in 1877, he argued, "it is characteristic of battle on the open sea that its sole goal is the annihilation of the enemy. Land battle offers other tactical possibilities, such as taking terrain, which do not exist in war at sea. Only annihilation can be accounted a success at sea."[14] This was a bold statement for a young lieutenant commander, but Tirpitz stuck to this conviction until the very end of his life.

Tirpitz had accompanied the Kaiser on an official trip to Great Britain in 1887, but their meeting in Kiel in the spring of 1891 proved important in their lives and to the future course of German and world history. There, at the Kaiser's suggestion, "a discussion took place as to how the navy should develop. The most varied views were expressed in the usual fashion, and without throwing any real light on the subject," Tirpitz remembered. The Kaiser, disappointed about this result, asked Tirpitz to develop his ideas. "So I described how I conceived the development of the navy, and as I had been continually jotting down my ideas on the subject, I was able to give a complete picture without any difficulty."[15]

Tirpitz, who had been appointed Chief of Staff of the Baltic Naval Station only the year before, became Chief of Staff of the naval High Command in Berlin in 1892. He fulfilled the task of developing the tactical work of the fleet with great enthusiasm, and it was during this time that he was given the nickname "master."[16] Tirpitz began to develop a doctrine of the strategic offensive that defined when and how battle should be sought under modern conditions, and what it could achieve.

The most famous of these is his service-memorandum, *Dienstschrift*, No. IX of 1894. The most important section is titled: "The Natural Purpose of a Fleet is the Strategic Offensive." Tirpitz states, "Those who consistently advocate the defensive often base their argument on the premise that the offensive enemy will present himself to do the decisive battle wherever that might suit us. This is however only the case to a very limited extent."[17] "The struggle for command of the sea," he wrote instead, "is the decisive phase [of naval war], and it will be decided in the main by battle, today as in all ages,"[18] To achieve command of the sea, a superiority of one-third was required.

Though Tirpitz did not mention Mahan, he used his language. Contrary to the memoranda he had written before, this *Dienstschrift* dealt with the tasks of the navy in a European war, and Germany's economic development and her future as a great power. This was an important twist in the development of Tirpitz's cast of mind. The Race for Africa and other unoccupied parts of the world had convinced him that a new partition of the globe was taking place. Only those who secured their share on time would be able to survive in the twentieth century.

This was a grand design, and though he did not mention Great Britain, it is clear that the fleet he wanted to build was directed against her. In his worldview, Britain had begun to play an increasingly more important role.

Despite the great prospects he opened, his grand design still met with opposition in naval circles. Many of his fellow officers regarded it as too bold and unsuitable for Germany's defense requirements. The Secretary of State for the Navy, Admiral Friedrich von Hollmann, refused to listen to these demands. Instead, following the Kaiser's wishes of a cruiser-fleet, he continued to ask for different types of cruisers, but not a homogenous battle fleet, which was to have a clearly defined task.

Due to Germany's peculiar geographical position and lack of a sufficient number of foreign stations, cruiser warfare was simply unsuitable for the navy. The members of the *Reichstag* were right in demanding a reunion of strategy with construction as a prerequisite of approving more money to finance Germany's defense needs. For several years the Emperor was unable to comply with these demands, for his naval advisers were divided over all questions dealing with construction and strategy. When the High Command had finally developed a long-term building plan for a battle fleet, the Imperial Navy Office again asked for cruisers, once more giving an example of incompetent naval planning.[19]

In the meantime, Tirpitz left Berlin for the Far East to take over command of the navy's East Asian Squadron. Despite his initial disappointment he seems to have enjoyed this command which took him up and down the Chinese coast and during which he identified the Bay of Kiachow as one of the places Germany should occupy in order to secure its claim in the event of a division of the Chinese Empire.

On March 31, 1897, he received a telegram ordering him to take over the Imperial Navy Office. Hollmann had again failed to convince the *Reichstag* of the Kaiser's naval plans. The Kaiser's dissatisfaction with the opposition of the *Reichstag* gave new impetus to the idea of changing the constitution fundamentally in order to strengthen his personal regime by force if need be. In this situation, Tirpitz was regarded as the only one to realize Wilhelm's plans of naval expansion. At first he hesitated, but eventually left the Far East for Berlin. For his own life as well as for the future of Germany and Europe Tirpitz's entry into the center of power was to have far-reaching consequences.

In the Center of Power

At the age of forty-eight, Tirpitz reached the center of power. The tasks he faced were huge. He had to put forward a revised version of a Navy Law that could pass the *Reichstag* and restore public confidence in the navy.

Having reached Berlin in early June, the new Secretary of State for the Navy presented his ideas to build up a powerful navy to the Kaiser. During his first audience, his *Immediatvortrag*, Tirpitz dismissed the Kaiser's and Admiral Büchsel's ideas on naval building in the meantime as "of no use."[1] In his eyes their proposals lacked strategic purpose. Instead, against the background of the rising antagonism between Germany and Great Britain, Tirpitz declared "the strengthening of our political might [and] importance against England" could be the only aim of a new naval bill.[2] Following the ideas he had developed in earlier years, Tirpitz emphasized the overall importance of battleships: "Since true success in cruiser war and transoceanic war against England is absolutely out of the question because of [our] lack of bases abroad and the geographic position of Germany, and since English naval officers, admiralty, etc., fully know this, then even politically it comes to a battleship war between Heligoland and the Thames."[3] This fleet, which was to challenge the Royal Navy on Britain's doorstep, was to consist of one double-squadron of twenty-one ship-of-the-line, eight coastal armored ships and thirty-six cruisers. As he had done before, he connected his proposals concerning the build-up of the navy with far-reaching political demands. The entire government should rally behind him, dissenting views in the navy should be suppressed, German foreign policy should be subordinated to the needs of the navy, and, finally, for financial reasons, the navy should also be given priority over the army. "The Emperor agreed immediately to my navy scheme, with a change of mind that surprised me,"[4] Tirpitz said in his *Memoirs*.

With the Kaiser's consent, Tirpitz immediately began to work out the details of the new navy bill. "Tirpitz soon proved that he was a man who knew what he wanted and how to achieve his aims. He had hardly settled at his desk when he told his subordinates that within six days they had to revise all the figures of the navy estimates for the fiscal year 1898–99, a task that normally would have taken a month. He also put up the first of many committees dealing with special tasks and problems. This committee was to work out the details of the Navy Law he wanted to introduce in the fall. Two days earlier he had already set up a new "Section for News and General Parliamentary Affairs." Under its director, *Korvettenkapitän* (Commander) August von Heeringen, the News Bureau had to establish close relations with the press, arrange publications of suitable articles, and create a favorable climate in German public opinion for a powerful fleet by reaching the most important and influential members of the society as well as the "broader masses" by widening their "limited horizon."[5]

Though Tirpitz with his bald head, forked beard, massive outward appearance and large, expressive eyes did not yet convey the impression of a commanding figure as he did in later years, all photographs taken in these months leave no doubt that he seemed to be a man of great self-confidence. For those in the inner circle and the public he appeared as a hard-working, strong-willed man who was full of energy and new ideas, trying "to deal with things which needed to be regarded in perspective from many sides," and to look for compromise where possible instead of stubbornly fighting open political battles. Tirpitz soon proved to be a skilful tactician in the field of political tactics.

However, if he was convinced that the fundamental principles of his program were in danger, he could fight like lion.

One of the secrets of Tirpitz's success was that he tried to guide his subordinates like a manager of a modern industrial enterprise instead of commanding them like a captain of a warship. "The transference of the brusque word of command (which is necessary in the face of the enemy) from the ship to the office and to big undertakings, the working with mere creatures who obey mechanically, the painful delimitation of departmental views, cripple the sense of responsibility and the capacity for making decisions, which are the chief requirements in military authorities," he wrote after the war.[6] Though he was in charge of naval politics and building, he wanted to be regarded only as "*primus inter pares*," for a successful organization can only be a team, he had told the Chief of the Naval Cabinet, Admiral Gustar von Senden, the year before.[7] In his memoirs, Tirpitz still proudly recalled the new working style he had introduced after he had been appointed Secretary of State: "My method of work always had Nelson's 'We are a band of brothers' for its motto." In his eyes his predecessors had tried to do everything themselves yet achieved nothing.

As a result he left the current business to his deputy and restricted himself to the preparation of the new navy bill. He gathered a group of young men around him helping to pave the way of the Navy Law through the *Reichstag*. For many of these men it was the beginning of a career in a navy which was soon to expand, offering them new opportunities and highest positions as either Chief of the Admiralty Staff or the Commander-in-Chief of the High Seas Fleet. While some of them remained loyal to their "master," others disagreed with him at some point and accordingly lost his confidence. Tirpitz demanded loyalty to himself as well as his ideas. He would never forgive anyone who challenged them.

This "band of brothers" prepared the final draft of the new navy bill. At the same time, the News Bureau carefully organized a campaign to gain support for it. Travelling all over Germany, its members spoke to important industrialists, politicians, and university professors. Journalists of all of Germany's leading newspapers were contacted directly or even invited to short trips on board of naval vessels. Their offices were flooded with official and semi-official statements as well as books on naval matters, statistics proving the necessity of building a navy, and photographs. In order to drown any protests against a new naval bill, the News Bureau also supported the campaigns of two important nationalistic societies, both the Colonial Society and the Pan German League, for an expansion of the navy, and helped pave the way for the foundation of another one in 1898, the important German Navy League which was to have one million members soon. More than 173 lectures on naval matters were organized in these months and 140,000 pamphlets were printed including more than two thousand copies of Alfred T. Mahan's *The Influence of Sea Power upon History.* University professors joined this campaign by either giving lectures or publishing articles emphasizing the need of a more powerful navy for geo-political or economic reasons. The Imperial Navy Office also organized tours to the waterside and exhibited the ships and the wharves. "We turned our attention to the schools," Tirpitz said, "Prizes were to be given by the Ministry of Education to the schools. [...] I was able [...] to carry out the whole of the campaign, without cost to the State, by means of voluntary contributions. This also was a new procedure in Germany: the decisive thing was that the idea caught on: then the spark spread of its own accord."[8]

In further efforts to rally support for a new navy bill, Tirpitz began to pay visits to many of Germany's princes, including the ageing Iron Chancellor, Prince Bismarck. Although Bismarck had no sympathy for *Weltpolitik*, he did not veto the plans. The Grand Duke of Baden, a "man provided with all the qualities of an old-time ruler, whose personality was far above average,"[9] even congratulated the Chancellor that "such an excellent personality had undertaken the advocacy of these great tasks, a man whose character and experience are equally splendid."[10] This statement shows that Tirpitz's new style of preparing his bills by trying to convince important decision-makers personally with his charm as well as with his great knowledge met with great approval after many years of chaos in the Imperial government.

Tirpitz owed his success to his own iron will, imagination, clever diplomatic handling of important decision and opinion makers within and without the government, and the men he had at his disposal in his own office. Unlike his predecessor, he could also count on the new Secretary of State for Foreign Affairs, the former German ambassador in

Rome, Bernhard von Bülow. Like Tirpitz, Bülow was one of the Kaiser's new young men, representing a complete turn around in German politics. Bülow was convinced that "only a successful foreign policy can help to reconcile, pacify, rally, unite."[11] Bülow also shared many of Tirpitz's social-darwinistic convictions on the rise and fall of nations and the role of navies in this process. "At all times the flourishing and thriving of a great state stands in closest connection to the development of their naval forces," he wrote to a leading industrialist in May 1898.[12] Since it was only a question of time before Bülow would replace the Chancellor, Prince Hohenlohe, the Secretary of State became Tirpitz's most important ally on the way into a great future.

On August 19, Tirpitz presented a draft of the new naval bill to the Kaiser. This draft was based on the proposals he had put forward during his audience in June and in his famous memorandum on the "General Considerations on the Constitution of our Fleet according to Ship Classes and Designs."[13] It again contained a number of important changes. Now the navy was to receive its full strength as early as 1905 instead of 1910. This decision increased cost and accelerated naval building from five to eleven battleships in the next seven years. Of course, economies in construction costs justified a more regular rate, but these measures show that Tirpitz's program was intrinsically expansive and put strong emphasis on the annual rate of construction. Only weeks after he had taken office, Tirpitz indicated that this law was the first step of expanding the navy to sixty ships-of-the-line and armored cruisers that would be automatically replaced after twenty years.[14] For the time being there was no need to demand more: "We cannot proceed more rapidly than we do; too much has been missed earlier and there has been too little system in our procedure. The latter is particularly bad. There is a lack of officers and continuous-service men. Almost worse is the absence of technical personnel. [...] There is a lack of shipyards and docks. There is a lack of industries for the creation and direction of the fleet. [...] Before we take the next forward step with our fleet, these wide gaps must be filled,"[15] he told an old friend in August. He had also not dropped any hint that might reveal his aim of building a fleet against Great Britain. Officially it was to be a sortie fleet, not a fleet that would make Germany a world power.

The Kaiser and the Chancellor agreed. In the following weeks, only a few changes were made to the draft of the bill. On October 29, 1897, the text of a "Law concerning the German Fleet" was presented to the Chamber of the States, the *Bundesrat*. This law fixed the strength of the German Fleet, the active life of the individual ship-classes, and committed the *Reichstag* to appropriate replacement funds automatically. It further covered the disposition and organization of the active fleet and the personnel required. All these stipulations served only one purpose: They were to make the navy independent from the *Reichstag*. Tirpitz was convinced that "only a formal Act could guarantee the ships being built within a specified time, and it alone could pull the navy out of the confusion, weakness, and critical condition generally into which it had been thrown before by its indifferent treatment by the *Reichstag*."[16] To make it acceptable for the *Reichstag*, Tirpitz made it look moderate and tried to persuade the *Reichstag* that the era of "zig-zag" naval policy was over. "It was hoped to get the Bill through the *Reichstag* in consideration of its being firmly founded on long years of work, so that the scheme presented itself as a reasoned demand, which had not been born in a moment but had inevitably evolved from experience."[17] Until 1905 the naval budget would not rise above 150 million marks annually, an increase of less than 30 percent on the total budget actually appropriated in March by the previous session of the *Reichstag*. Similarly the clarity of the law seemed also commendable. "The navy knew where it was going and how it intended to get there," one historian has rightly remarked,[18] and Bülow, Tirpitz's closest ally in the new government wrote in his *Memoirs*: "An entirely different wind blew from this Bill than from all the earlier naval Bill. A clear spirit and a strong will spoke through it. The entire project and all its provisions were of the same stuff."[19]

Tirpitz could be proud of what he had achieved in less than six months: The Kaiser was about to get his fleet while the *Bundesrat* and *Reichstag* received a bill that put an end to "limitless fleet-plans." The Imperial government seemed to move into quieter waters after years of conflict both with the Kaiser and parliament on the naval question. Owing to Tirpitz's efforts, an increasing number of people seemed to understand the linking of naval power to economic power and the equation of economic power with political power.

On November 30, the Kaiser opened the new session of the *Reichstag* with a speech in which he voiced many of Tirpitz's arguments. "The development of our battle fleet has not kept up with the tasks with which Germany is compelled to present to its maritime force. Our fleet is not sufficiently strong to secure our homeports and waters in the event of hostilities and to prevent a blockade or extensive operations by the enemy. It has not kept up with the lively growth of our overseas interests," he declared. He also emphasized the defensive nature of the proposed navy bill maintaining that it only intended to "assert German prestige in the eyes of the people of the world."[20]

Though the Kaiser's speech received much applause, Tirpitz was not certain that the Navy Law would pass the *Reichstag* in its present form. Despite all his endeavors, it was still not unlikely that the *Reichstag* would reject the clauses concerning its right of annually reviewing appropriations. Tirpitz thought that some members of the government had secretly offered a compromise on this important aspect of the Navy Law thus impeding his position. Tirpitz clarified that he was willing to fight if necessary. Whether dissolution of the *Reichstag* would have changed the situation is uncertain; his harsh reaction helped to close ranks. Tirpitz invited a number of leading deputies to his office at the *Leipzigerplatz* to discuss the bill frankly and in a free atmosphere. In these talks he revealed qualities that a leading conservative, Count Westarp, still admired thirty years later: "Tirpitz was a master in his psychological dealings with deputies to reach his patriotic goals. Unlike Bülow, he did not resort to coarse flattering; he rather knew how to empathize with the nature and motivations of deputies and parties."[21]

On December 6, the first reading of the bill in the *Reichstag* began. The Chancellor emphasized that the Fleet Law "demonstrates that a policy of adventure is far from our minds," but he also stressed that "in maritime questions, Germany must be able to speak a modest, above all, a wholly German word."[22] Then Tirpitz gave his maiden speech: "Our fleet has the function of a protective fleet. It changes its character not one bit as a result of this law." Fully confident of his arguments, he spoke "as if the passage of the law were a mere technical detail which reasonable men could fix up in an afternoon. Obviously any sensible man could see that if the *Reichstag* set the effective fighting strength of the navy by law, there would be no more talk of limitless fleet plans."[23]

Bülow, the new Secretary for Foreign Affairs, also supported the law in a speech: "We do not by any means feel the need to stick our finger in every pie, but on the other hand [...] the days when the German happily surrendered the land to one of his neighbours, to another the sea, and reserved for himself the heavens, where pure doctrine was enthroned [...] Those days are over. [...] In a word, we don't want to put anyone in the shade, but we too demand our place in the sun." [24]

Tirpitz successfully defended the bill against all its critics. Contrary to Bülow, he was no brilliant speaker, but his arguments were convincing. In order to keep up the pressure on the *Reichstag*, he had continued to mobilize those who had a direct or an indirect interest in the navy. In mid-January 1898 a group of leading businessmen and industrialists passed a resolution that unanimously supported the navy bill. The message was clear: They should regard it "as a sign of the way the affairs of the business community, that is, trade policy and the fleet, are to be treated in the future,"[25] as a liberal newspaper put it. This support, however, did not mean that industrialists and other vested interests could in any way influence his program. Throughout his time in office, Tirpitz remained a shrewd businessman who haggled down armor and ship prices as much as possible even at the danger of risking serious conflicts with influential industrial enterprises like Germany's most important armament contractor, the Krupp works in Essen.

In the end Tirpitz had to accept only one alteration of the draft proposed by the Center Party, one of his most important political allies in the *Reichstag* in the build-up of the navy. He had to accept "a financial limit to make it more palatable to the *Reichstag*," a fact "which soon created many difficulties, because the value of money depreciated steadily."[26] In return, the Center Party proposed shortening the length of the law from seven to six years. Tirpitz got his fleet earlier than expected.

When the *Reichstag* passed the last paragraph of the Navy Law on March 26, 1898, Tirpitz had achieved the impossible. He had liberated the navy from the *Reichstag*, enhanced Germany's political importance towards Great Britain, and caused people to begin accepting the idea of a symbiotic relationship between sea power and the growth of sea interests. The Kaiser rewarded him by appointing him a member of the Prussian Ministry of State, placing him in a position of power shared only by the Chancellor, the Foreign Secretary, and the Secretary of the Interior.

Tirpitz began to consider the possibility of further increasing the fleet before the expiration of the existing Navy Law in 1903. He intended to stabilize a building rate of three capital ships a year. The Navy Law had secured this tempo only until 1900. He first proposed a new increase of the fleet to the Kaiser as early as November 1898. Having toyed with different ideas of how to realize this aim, in September 1899, he revealed his further plans: "The statement of Salisbury: great states become greater and stronger and small states become smaller and weaker [is] also my view," he told the Kaiser. "Since Germany has remained particularly backwards in respect to sea power, it is a vital question for Germany as a world power and *Kulturstaat* to catch up with what has been missed. Both because sea power has to be established in the narrowest sense (fleet) and preserved as such and because power is important in itself, Germany must keep her population German and develop herself further as an industrial and commercial world power. In the latter lies at present the strongest means for keeping the surplus population German. The development of Germany into an industrial and commercial power is irresistible like a law of nature. If one wanted to dam Germany in, the development would none the less continue. [...] In the case of such commercial and industrial development, points of contact and conflict with other nations increase. Naval power is essential if Germany does not want to go under."[27] In order to achieve this aim he demanded the introduction of a new fleet bill that doubled the existing fleet. "As soon as the aim is reached, Your Majesty has an effective strength of forty-five ships of the line with complete accessories—so powerful [...] that only England will be superior. But also against England we undoubtedly have good chances through geographical position, military system, torpedo boats, tactical training, planned organizational development, and leadership united by the monarch. Apart from our by no means hopeless conditions of fighting, England will have lost [any] political or economic [...] inclination to attack us and will as a result concede to your Majesty sufficient naval presence (*Seegeltung*) [...] for the conduct of a grand policy overseas."[28]

To Tirpitz's displeasure, the Kaiser announced the introduction of a new bill only a fortnight later in a speech in Hamburg. Although Tirpitz had not finished his preparations yet, he had no choice but to take this opportunity and introduce the new navy bill early. The British seizure of a German steamer off the South African coast in December, "introduced an element of national feeling into the pro-Boer enthusiasm" of the public, which facilitated the introduction of a new bill.

The new bill passed in June 1900 was a great success. Though he had given up his demand for six large armored cruisers, he had used the public's anti-English sentiment to justify doubling the strength of the German Navy: "It is not necessary that the battle fleet at home is equal to that of the greatest naval power. In general this naval power would not be in a position to concentrate its entire naval forces against us. Even if it succeeds in encountering us with a superior force, the destruction of the German fleet would so much damage the enemy that his own position as a world power would be brought into question."[29] This was the famous "risk theory" which was to deter Great Britain from any attack on its new rival in the world. Similarly important, Tirpitz had been able to tie the hands of the *Reichstag* politically and financially for the future, for the latter had accepted Tirpitz's idea of a fleet that automatically renewed itself. "By this *Lex Imperfecta* as represented by the second Navy Bill, which was binding as regards matériel, but allowed a free hand as regards finance, the *Reichstag* surrendered the possibility of refusing money for the new types of vessels, which were increasing in size and cost unless it was prepared to bring on itself the reproach of building inferior ships. Thus, in 1900 the *Reichstag* decided by legal enactment to carry out the naval scheme which had been drawn up, and bound itself morally to create no more financial difficulties for us [...]."[30] Tirpitz, however, was not only successful in naval politics. In December 1899, he was promoted to the rank of vice-admiral and on January 1 he and his family had been ennobled.

It is clear that neither the Kaiser's "naval passion" nor his pressure to enlarge the navy, nor Tirpitz's shrewdness can sufficiently explain the shift in German politics as well as in military thinking in the 1890s. It seems unlikely that they would have been successful if the importance of sea power had not been realized by a steadily increasing number of people. There can be no doubt that many contemporaries were proud of their political, economic, and military achievements since the unification: Between 1871 and 1895 the German population had risen from 41 to 52 million; GNP had risen from 14.6 to 27.6 billion marks, exports had increased from 2.9 in 1880 to 3.6 billion in 1897, imports from 2.8 to 4.6 billion marks. They had good reason to believe that Imperial Germany was a vigorous young nation. The ideas of imperialism and the political and military events in East Asia as well as in other distant parts of the world in the mid-1890s had further enhanced the conviction that Germany had to become a world power in order to preserve its achievements. Many contemporaries did not share the harsh tone of many of the Kaiser's speeches, but they shared his message: "in distant areas [beyond the ocean], no important decision should be taken without Germany and the German Emperor."[31] The ideas of Alfred T. Mahan and Tirpitz's proposals seemed to offer a means to realize this aim. Traditional concepts of power politics and social-Darwinist ideas had formed a symbiosis. Bülow wrote to a leading German industrialist, Friedrich A. Krupp in 1898, the "flowering and prospering of great states is closely connected with the development of their naval forces."[32] A naval presence, *Seegeltung* was allegedly a prerequisite for the protection of the German colonies, and of economic wealth, industrial progress, and commerce. Without a strong navy, Tirpitz argued, Germany would be unable to preserve its steadily rising "sea interests," *Seeinteressen*, and decline to the status of a pre-industrial, "poor agricultural state."[33]

Tirpitz's propaganda campaign, the lectures given by more than two-hundred "fleet professors," the speeches and articles by bourgeois politicians, and the enthusiasm with which thousands of people visited the fleet in the country's naval stations were genuine expressions of the convictions and feelings of many people in Germany at the turn of the last century.

Tirpitz, Bülow, and the Kaiser represented these feelings and convictions, and tried to make them correspond with their own notions of power politics, the rise and fall of nations, or of a personal regime. In spite of the vagueness of the German demand for equal entitlement, "*Gleichberechtigung*," the Imperial government knew what it wanted. Tirpitz always maintained that a powerful navy would greatly enhance

Germany's alliance value, *Bündnisfähigkeit*, and strengthen the nation's position in the emerging new world power system. In truth, he, Bülow, and the Kaiser, however, wanted to revolutionize the international system by replacing the *Pax Britannica* with a *Pax Germanica* "The leading German statesmen, and above all Kaiser Wilhelm, have looked into the distant future and are striving to make Germany's already swiftly-growing position as a world power into a dominating one, reckoning hereby upon becoming the genial successor to England in this respect. People in Berlin are however well aware that Germany would not be in the position today or for a long time to assume this succession, and for this reason a speedy collapse of English world power is not desired since it is fully recognised that Germany's far-reaching plans are at present only castles in the air. Notwithstanding this, Germany is already preparing with speed and vigour for her self-appointed future mission. In this connection I may permit myself to refer to the constant concern for the growth of German naval forces [...] England is now regarded as the most dangerous enemy which, at least as long as Germany is not sufficiently armed at sea, must be treated with consideration in all ways [...] but because of the universally dominant Anglophobia, it is not easy [to convince public opinion of this],"[34] the Austrian ambassador reported in May 1900.

Against this background it is difficult to regard the risk theory only as "a defensive deterrent concept."[35] Though Tirpitz never fully revealed his ultimate aims, historian Volker Berghahn rightly argued that Tirpitz wanted to establish a ratio of 2:3 in battleships between Germany and Britain. Tirpitz "preferred to rely on the deterrent value of his battle fleet rather than become involved in a risky war with Great Britain, but the Imperial Navy was designed to be more than a deterrent in the narrow sense of the word; it was to be used for a policy of diplomatic bullying."[37] Britain's well-known problems with its navy would give the Kaiser's navy a realistic chance in a battle with a fleet that was numerically superior by a factor of one third. Since Tirpitz was convinced that Britain could not build more than ninety battleships, he planned a fleet consisting of sixty similar vessels to achieve "fair play" or to fight for superiority even if this meant self-destruction.

In order to ensure his long-term plans for this fleet were not thwarted by the *Reichstag*'s refusal to appropriate funds to build the ships, Tirpitz tried to make the navy independent by stipulating in the first Navy Law that all ships, which were built at a rate of three capital ships a year, had to be replaced by newly built vessels after twenty years. Thus, the Kaiser would have a powerful navy of sixty capital ships always at his disposal. The history of the relationship between the army and parliament illustrates that this aspect had important political implications, namely the restriction of parliamentary influence on traditional royal prerogatives. These prerogatives were important safeguards of the existing order. In contrast to the modernity of its industrial system, the German political and social order was pre-modern in many ways. The military, the bureaucracy, and the diplomatic service were still parts of the traditional monarchical prerogative on which the *Reichstag* had almost no influence. Moreover, in spite of their decreasing economic importance in a quickly industrializing country, the old agrarian elites still exerted more political influence on the development of the state and society than seemed justified. After all other measures had failed in the past, the government hoped that sea power, and the great success in world politics, would safeguard the overall expansion of German industry, foreign trade, colonies, and the navy, and offer a permanent solution to the social problem which threatened the existing political and social order. To what extent Tirpitz was a social-imperialist and to what extent he only wanted to save the navy from parliamentary intervention is difficult to decide. He felt, however, deeply committed to the Bismarckian constitution with its authoritarian, anti-democratic, and anti-parliamentarian tendencies. Only this constitution seemed to secure stability at home, economic progress, and, above all, an assertive foreign policy.[37]

This was indeed an ambitious plan which was supposed to be put into reality in stages; and even though its flaws—Germany's geographical position and its limited financial resources, the danger of costly technological developments as well as instability of the international system, the impossibility of permanently manipulating the masses on a large scale and the increasing speed of social and political change at home—are so obvious from hindsight, the evidence is very strong that Tirpitz had a consistent plan after taking office in 1897. Moreover, at least for the time Bülow and the Kaiser supported his plan.

For the time being Tirpitz, Bülow, and the Kaiser had every reason to be satisfied with what they had achieved. Britain even asked for an alliance with Germany due to its deteriorating international position during the Boer War, and in domestic politics conservative agrarians and liberals compromised on the difficult question of a new tariff on agrarian imports.

For Tirpitz the years which followed were more peaceful. The next *Novelle* to stabilize a building rate of three ships a year was not due until 1905–06. In 1903, he began planning to build a third double-squadron, thus increasing the navy's strength in capital ships from sixty to eighty. In order to not overstrain the budget, Tirpitz dropped this idea and decided to introduce only a small *Novelle* in 1905–06, demanding the vessels he had had to strike from his original draft in 1900: six large cruisers.

This decision was wise because contrary to Tirpitz's expectations, the international system had begun to change to Germany's disadvantage. Britain had begun to conclude alliances with its rivals in order to settle long-lasting conflicts and save money on defense spending. Japan's defeat of Russia had further complicated international relations. Germany only could rely on one ally, Austria-Hungary, once Anglo-German relations began to deteriorate.

Tirpitz advised moderation and patience. He had always warned of the danger zone Germany had to pass until the Fleet had reached its full strength. After a meeting discussing a Russian alliance offer, he wrote to the Foreign Secretary: "We should not undertake the conclusion of a political treaty for the present, but await events. On the whole, our most important political object is to gain time and to build our fleet."[38] This seemed even more necessary since even many of his collaborators now warned him that the initial assumption that peace could be preserved until the navy was completed was no longer tenable. Britain had realized what was going on across the North Sea and was making it increasingly difficult to pass the danger zone. Any wrong move might prove disastrous now.

Time was running out. In 1905–06, Bülow attempted to split the entente between France and Great Britain. Instead, both partners allied against Germany. In 1907, Russia also became a partner of this system.

Although Bülow, Tirpitz, and many contemporaries regarded this system as a deliberate encirclement of Germany, it was actually an attempt to protect themselves against Germany's incalculable aspirations.

Tirpitz's assumptions about finance, domestic politics, and technological developments were also wrong. The most important development was the technological change in shipbuilding with its impact on the size of warships, the thickness of their armor, the calibers of their guns, and their speed. All these changes entailed a steady rise in costs—a mortal blow to Tirpitz's plan.

The driving force in this respect was Tirpitz's opponent on the opposite side of the North Sea, Admiral John Fisher, First Sea Lord since 1904. Fisher redistributed the ships of the Royal Navy, concentrating the majority of them in home waters now. He also began building a completely new type of warship, which was much bigger, more powerful, and faster than its predecessors: HMS *Dreadnought*. Though Fisher's measures were not primarily directed against Germany, Tirpitz regarded them as a direct challenge and immediately followed Fisher's revolution in naval construction.

Far-reaching changes in battleship construction had been imminent since 1903–04. The Kaiser had tried to urge Tirpitz to change the principles of construction for many months.

In spite of Tirpitz's reservations for principle reasons, German naval planners had begun working on the construction of bigger and more powerful ships. In 1904 they had discussed plans for a ship of 15,000 tons, armed with ten 28 cm guns. However, Tirpitz did not accept it, for the leap seemed incompatible with a number of technical and financial aspects of his program. Big ships would have difficulty passing the Kiel Canal. Moreover, any leap would make him vulnerable to accusations in the *Reichstag* that the navy was again pursuing "limitless fleet-plans."

Whatever reservations Tirpitz may have had, the reports of the German naval attaché in London confirmed that the Royal Navy had decided to make the leap he had tried to avoid, and that he had no option but follow if he ever wanted to reach his aims. Tirpitz accepted the design of a battleship displacing 15,700 tons and armed with eight 28 cm guns in March 1905. This design of Germany's first all-big-gun ship was to change many times; when SMS *Nassau* was launched in March 1908, it displaced almost 19,000 tons and it was armed with twelve 28 cm guns, two big guns more than HMS *Dreadnought* had had when it had been launched in 1906.

The consequences of Tirpitz's decision to accept Fisher's challenge were far-reaching. Completely new designs were necessary. Any change in one respect would cause changes in other respects. Second, harbor installations, the Kiel Canal, and docks had to be enlarged. Third, he had to convince the *Reichstag* and the public of the need of providing more money to execute the naval program. Fourth, the fact that Great Britain had now responded to the German challenge would have an enormous impact on Germany's position among the Great Powers, for it was very likely that Great Britain would do whatever possible to improve its position against Germany. Fifth, Fisher's naval revolution would also question Tirpitz's strategic principles and tactical doctrines, for the bigger and more valuable the ships became the more dangerous and this means the less probable a decisive battle would become especially if alternatives like a distant blockade instead of a close blockade were similarly effective strategies. Sixth, industry had to adjust its facilities to the requirements of the new "capital ships" as the battleship and the battle cruiser were soon to be called.

Tirpitz was aware of many of these problems, but he accepted the challenges; he was convinced that he had a good chance of winning the race against Fisher—who would start anew from "point zero." As Holger Herwig said, it "speaks volumes for the nature of the decision-making process in Wilhelmian Germany that the British challenge was accepted without input from the chancery, the foreign office, the treasury, or the two agencies directly responsible for naval strategic planning, the admiralty staff and the High Seas Fleet!"[39]

Tirpitz also anticipated and accepted the risks he was taking. In September 1906, he informed the Kaiser about the decision that German battle-cruisers would be armed with 28 cm guns and that he anticipated a deterioration of Anglo-German relations: "The English have seen that with their action with the *Dreadnought* in the previous spring they made a mistake in the face of Germany and are angry about it. This annoyance will increase as they see that we follow them immediately with large cruisers, all the more so, as ours will be somewhat larger than *Invincible*."[40] He ignored Bülow's warning to keep down expenditures until new sources of revenue had been found.[41] Bülow anticipated that Tirpitz might be able to keep up with Fisher as far as quantity and quality were concerned, but that he might lose the race on the domestic front where any new burden on the taxpayer from the lower classes would increase the number of Social Democratic voters in the next general election and undermine the social stability they had hoped to achieve through an offensive naval policy.

Tirpitz was successful in constructing the battleships and battle cruisers. The four ships of the *Nassau* class and the first German battle cruiser were launched in 1908–09. Generally speaking, underwater protection was excellent, but the mounting of the six turrets of *Nassau*'s main armament made them inferior to the British battleships because they did not have turbines and could not bring a maximum number of arms to bear.

The design of Germany's future *Dreadnought* ships followed similar patterns. Generally speaking they were known for their smaller caliber guns, their thicker armor and their slower speed. Nevertheless the navy was convinced that they could still match their rivals. In 1913, the *Bayern* class displaced 28,600 tons, reached a speed of 22 knots, and had 38 cm guns arranged in super-firing, raised twin turrets fore and aft. They were equal to the ships of the *Queen Elizabeth* class, and the prototype of modern battleships for the next twenty years to come. The intention to equip German capital ships with diesel engines would soon revolutionize both shipbuilding and naval strategy.

This brief sketch of German shipbuilding under Tirpitz cannot disguise the increasing difficulties he had to face. He built the ships and introduced two new navy bills, *Novellen*, into the *Reichstag* in 1906 and 1908. Both were passed almost unanimously and increased the navy's strength and ship quality. In 1905–06 naval enthusiasts demanded more ships, risking a *Copenhagening* of the fleet and undermining the basic principles of his plan. The Navy League proved difficult to restrain in its attempts to push him forward.

Tirpitz enjoyed the full support of his band of brothers and the Kaiser, who loved his navy and was ready to fulfill his dream of Germany becoming the world's leading sea power. In 1899, the Kaiser dissolved the High Command of the Navy at Tirpitz's request, strengthening his influence within the navy. He intervened when internal critics questioned Tirpitz's course and until the outbreak of war, supported his policy without reservations.

The Kaiser's support proved essential in the years of crises. The introduction of a new navy bill in 1907–08, which accelerated naval shipbuilding while the Royal Navy slowed its building program, had been the turning point from the British point of view. Anglo-German relations quickly deteriorated over the fleet question. The German ambassador in London, Count Paul von Metternich, warned the government in Berlin of the disastrous effects of naval building on Anglo-German relations. In the summer of 1908, these tense relations caused the Chief of the Admiralty Staff to fear a pre-emptive strike against the High Seas Fleet.

In spite of the fact that the new navy bill had passed the *Reichstag* with little opposition, Tirpitz watched this development with concern and suspicion. He had realized that contrary to the demands of the Navy League "a faster increase [of the navy] was hardly possible without overstraining the bow. The steady development is the greatest [part] in it and provides the most secure guarantee for the future."[42] Thus, he could not help feeling that the tide was turning. The reports of the German ambassador in London seemed to contribute to "a decline of sentiment for the fleet."[43]

For the time being he was convinced that he could still count on the Kaiser and the Chancellor. In February, in order to alleviate anti-German feelings in Britain, the Kaiser wrote to the First Lord of the Admiralty, Lord Tweedmouth, claiming, "the German Naval Bill is not aimed at England and is not a 'Challenge to British Supremacy of the Sea,' which will remain unchallenged to generations to come."[44] This caused a great public stir because it showed that the Kaiser still supported Tirpitz unconditionally. Only a few months later, the Kaiser met with Foreign Office official, Lord Charles Hardinge, to discuss the matter again. When Lord Hardinge appealed to him: "You must stop or build slower," The Kaiser said: "Then we shall fight for it is a question of national honour and dignity."[45]

While the Kaiser stuck to Tirpitz's naval program, Bülow changed his mind. Unlike the Kaiser and Tirpitz, he realized that Germany could not afford the strongest army and the second strongest navy in Europe. He was also convinced that a further rise of tensions could prove detrimental to the nation's freedom of action in international politics. Most importantly, he emphasized the importance of the army: "We cannot weaken the army, for our destiny will be decided on land."[46]

With Anglo-German relations deteriorating and the impending Bosnian crisis impairing Germo-Russo relations, Bülow asked Tirpitz if "Germany and the German people could calmly and with confidence envisage an English attack?"[47]

This was a severe blow and disappointment to Tirpitz. "Bülow has deserted me,"[48] he remembered in December 1912. Tirpitz could not affirm Bülow's question, but he refused to agree that the naval question rather than commercial rivalry lay at the root of the conflict. Tirpitz argued that only constant pressure of a formidable fleet of battle ships could force Britain to make concessions to Germany. "In a few years our fleet would be so strong that an attack on it even by Britain would mean a great military risk."[49] The Chancellor tried to exploit this weak point in Tirpitz's chain of arguments by trying to convince him of the political advantages of a naval agreement and a shift from battleship building to a *Kleinkrieg*-strategy based on the extensive use of mines, submarines, and coastal defense. Tirpitz rejected the *Kleinkrieg*-concept: "We can double and triple our torpedo-boat system and submarines, we can spike our entire coast with cannon, but this part of our naval power can in no way have a pacific influence. Without a battle fleet we would be exposed to every insolence on the part of England."[50] Tirpitz pleaded for an open arms race and warned Bülow that any concessions were only an indication of capitulation before British threats and of German humiliation. Though he admitted, "our situation in the face of England was very serious," he maintained "the lesser danger of war for us existed in perseverance and that giving in would in spite of the connected humiliation of Germany only increase the danger."[51]

Since Tirpitz threatened with his resignation, Bülow could not challenge him openly, but he continued to pressure him. "If Tirpitz considers this route to be correct, he should go to England to negotiate it,"[52]

Bülow wrote after reading Tirpitz's proposals for a naval agreement. These attempts to change the course of both German foreign policy and German naval policy were to no avail. Even the Navy Scare in Britain caused by accusations that Germany had secretly accelerated its building rate—a fact that Tirpitz had to admit—did not cause Tirpitz to change his mind. With the Kaiser's support, he refused to yield in any respect.

In April Bülow argued that "he could no longer take the responsibility [...] we would now throughout the world have England as an enemy [...] who would use the first opportunity to attack us with other powers. It could be after two years, as soon as the reorganization of the Russian army was completed."[53] He warned the members of this conference: "The only black cloud lies over the North Sea, but this one might cause a thunderstorm."[54]

On each occasion Tirpitz remained stubborn, arguing that "the danger zone in our relationship with England would be overcome in five to six years." When the first new battleships were commissioned in two years, Germany would be considerably stronger than it was now. These arguments, however did not answer Bülow's question of how the current danger could be overcome. For fear of any misunderstandings, Tirpitz refused both to draft a formula and to take the initiative.

Three weeks later Bülow resigned. He had failed to win a majority in the *Reichstag* for a financial reform that was necessary due to the rising costs of Tirpitz's naval program. The conservatives rejected a bill introducing an inheritance tax, which was supposed to increase the government's financial resources. Instead, the government again had to put the burden on the "little man" by raising new indirect taxes. In many ways it was an irony of history and an indication of the fundamental differences between the German and the British political system that, at the same time, the British government even risked challenging the House of Lords with Lloyd George's *Peoples' Budget* in order to finance out-building the German navy.

The new Chancellor, Theodor von Bethmann Hollweg, also regarded a détente with Britain as necessary. With the Kaiser's approval, he took up negotiations with the British ambassador in Berlin, Lord George

Goschen. This time Tirpitz was willing to take the initiative and negotiate an agreement.

In spring 1909, Tirpitz realized that Germany could not out-build Britain with its enormous financial resources. Instead of once again reducing the building-rate of capital ships as in 1907–1908 and 1908–1909, the British cabinet finally decided to double the German building-tempo of four capital ships by laying down eight in 1909–1910 to defend Britain's naval supremacy against Germany.

For Tirpitz, this unexpected great increase in British naval building was an incentive to try to bind Britain by an agreement that included a ratio of the two fleets that was more favorable to the German than the British navy. According to his proposals the ratio would in fact have been 3:4 as far as modern ships of the Dreadnought were concerned—an offer which Britain would hardly accept.

The new Chancellor thwarted this attempt by letting Tirpitz know that he expected proposals that would not impede negotiations before they had begun. Tirpitz changed his proposals and the respective ratios several times in the course of intergovernmental negotiations, but the prospects for these negotiations were bleak. Until the outbreak of war, Tirpitz would suspect that the Chancellor might sacrifice the fleet for better Anglo-German relations. Accordingly, he always took great care that Bethmann Hollweg established no link between both the envisaged naval and the political agreement. Tirpitz knew that he faced either disaster or triumph. Any agreement, unless it contained substantial British concessions as far as the strength of the Royal Navy was concerned, was likely to prove disadvantageous for the German navy somehow. The Navy Law's stipulations about the size of the fleet and the building rate of its vessels were the foundation of Tirpitz's naval policy. In his opinion, any change would impede his final aim of building a fleet that would be able to finally gain command of the sea. Against the background of increasingly scarce financial resources it was also likely that the navy might sooner or later lose its priority in defense spending to the army. Moreover, Tirpitz was afraid that admitting a smaller navy or a slower building-rate would be sufficient to achieve its aims, the Imperial Government would immediately face disastrous protests. The left would argue that huge sums had been wasted; the right would accuse the government of giving up its aim of acquiring a place in the sun. "If we ourselves undermine the Navy Law which is already in great danger due to the whole situation, we do not know where the journey is going to take us to," he wrote in September 1909.[55]

These considerations were the crux of the problem. Whereas only a substantial reduction of Germany's building program or building rate might be a sufficient incentive for Britain to discuss an agreement, after the costly build-up of the navy, only a British declaration of neutrality in the event of war on the continent would have been regarded as an acceptable price.

Since Germany regarded a political agreement as a prerequisite of a naval agreement while Britain wanted to conclude a naval agreement first and make vague promises later, these negotiations never made any progress. Even though both sides finally agreed to negotiate both agreements simultaneously, this never happened. Morevoer, Britain soon lost interest in a naval agreement for she knew that per the Navy Law, the German building rate would go down from four to two capital ships a year in 1912 anyway. Tirpitz, in return, was also unwilling to renounce his ability to introduce a new Novelle to stabilize a continuous building-rate of three ships a year. He told the Kaiser during an *Immediatvortrag* in October 1910: "Because it is the backbone of Your Majesty's naval policy that the German fleet must be so strong that a British attack becomes a risky undertaking. The position of the German Empire as a world power rests on this risk, as does the effect our fleet has in maintaining the peace."

The main reason for Tirpitz's pessimistic view of the future development of German naval politics was the fact that the new Secretary of State for the Treasury "surrounded the treasury with barbed-wire", as he remembered in 1919. "I have had to fight for the most necessary grants until I was tired out, less with the *Reichstag*, which evinced growing insight, than with the Secretary of the Imperial Treasury and with the Imperial Chancellor, who, the one blinded by departmental fanaticism, the other by political dreams, suppressed a great deal that was desirable for Germany's armament during those years, because, as they said, Germany had no money to spare for this purpose."[56]

However, even high-ranking officers in the navy began to question his course. Since Tirpitz invested all resources into the build-up of the fleet, money was increasingly lacking for other urgent needs like higher pay and training crews. Tensions between him and the "front," as he called the rest of the navy, rose when his rival Admiral Henning von Holtzendorff was appointed Commander-in-Chief of the High Seas Fleet in 1909. Holtzendorff questioned Tirpitz's strategic concept and the principles of his naval program. In 1911 he even openly supported the Chancellor's attempts to prevent the introduction of a new supplement, *Novelle*, to the Navy Law.

For Tirpitz, it was a stroke of luck that the Chancellor's attempt to assert Germany's role in the world by embarking on an offensive policy against the intervention of France in Morocco in 1911 ended in a complete political disaster. Contrary to his intentions, the Chancellor thus renewed suspicions of German foreign policy. In order to prevent a German attack on France, the liberal cabinet decided to put the Royal Navy on alert as well as to intensify its military talks with France. On July 21, 1911, the Chancellor of the Exchequer, David Lloyd George, officially warned the German government that Britain would not remain neutral in the event of a Franco-German war.

Though it is unlikely that the Chancellor wanted to risk a European war, he had underestimated the repercussions his offensive political strategy on France's entente partner. Moreover, instead of gaining a political success, which might even influence the outcome of the forthcoming general election in January 1912, the government would face serious troubles on the domestic front.

Tirpitz, who had not been involved in this decision, watched the events with rising concern. From his point of view, Lloyd George's warning was a blessing. Whereas the government pursued a more careful course for fear of an untimely continental war, parts of the public were outraged by this renewed British attempt to thwart Germany's attempts to find a "place in the sun."

Tirpitz put forward his idea of introducing a new *Novelle* to the Fleet Law as early as late August. Arguing that the political defeat had seriously damaged Germany's political prestige, he asked the Chancellor for an additional six large ships to stabilize an annual building rate of three ships a year and to form a third active squadron. "For a State," he later claimed, "which is conscious that the welfare of its citizens does not consist in extenuation, but in power and prestige, there is only one means of restoring its reputation if it wants to avoid war: that is, to show that it is not afraid, and at the same time to strengthen its protection against a defeat when serious trouble seems imminent."[57] A *Novelle* would also strengthen the position of the government, for it would help to rally the conservative as well as the bourgeois parties behind it and thus "take the wind out of the social-democratic and left-liberal parties."[58]

For the first time Tirpitz met with strong opposition from the Chancellor who was afraid that a *Novelle* would destroy all hopes of improving Anglo-German relations, and even mean war. Tirpitz's proposals would increase Germany's war-preparedness and its fighting strength. Bethmann Hollweg did not share Tirpitz's assertion that "it was wholly impossible for England to make a *casus belli* out of the Supplementary Bill [*Novelle*] after the settlement of the Morocco negotiations."[59]

Tirpitz again counted on the Kaiser. He was able to convince him of the need of a new navy bill. Against the background of continuously rising costs of battleships and battle cruisers, Tirpitz argued that the *Reichstag* might be unwilling to appropriate the funds necessary to increase the building-rate from two to three ships a year in 1918. As a result, instead of sixty the Kaiser would only have forty capital ships at his disposal in the future. Tirpitz also emphasized the political aspects of the *Novelle*. "Without an "adequate defensive chance against an English attack our policy must always show consideration for England and our sacrifices would have been in vain," he told the Kaiser. In that case, "history would condemn German naval policy as a complete failure." In his eyes, the only means to avoid this fiasco was to conclude an agreement establishing a power relationship of 2:3 between the German and the British navy. This would guarantee Germany's security without threatening Britain. "If England accepts the proposal, Germany will be free to reach the [2:3] ratio by means of another naval bill." If, on the other hand, "England refuses, she will have to bear the stigma [of refusal] and cannot make any complaints." "There can be no better start for the present and no better foundation for the future in my opinion," he concluded.[60]

Convinced that Britain would accept an agreement on this basis due to its financial situation, the Kaiser approved Tirpitz's proposals of introducing a new *Novelle* and making an official offer to Britain in the *Reichstag*. "An increase of the navy was," he wrote to the Chancellor, "a question of vital importance to the future foreign policy of the Empire."[61]

It was unlikely that Britain would accept Tirpitz's proposals after it had rejected them as incompatible with its own defense policy in the negotiations before. Tirpitz thought that only a strong navy, which automatically renewed itself at a rate of three capital ships, could enhance Germany's position towards Great Britain decisively. Since the situation seemed favorable to reach this aim, the end justified all means, even if this meant a continuation of the cold war between Britain and Germany for the time being. "The events of the past summer have in my opinion indeed shown clearly that the danger of war has come closer if Germany is still to conduct an active world policy, all the more so as England has clearly shown that she would actively participate in a Franco-German war,"[62] he argued in a letter to the Chancellor. He continued: "When the current naval policy was embarked on all relevant decision-making factors were clear about the fact the we would have to pass through a danger zone. Then [as now] the ultimate question was: either to abdicate as a world power or to take risks."[63] Tirpitz was willing to take these risks at any cost.

In spite of the Kaiser's support, Tirpitz had difficulty achieving his aim. The Chancellor, the Chancellor of the Exchequer, and the German ambassador in London stubbornly resisted the introduction of a navy bill. Bethmann Hollweg feared a conflict with Great Britain and the repercussions of a *Novelle* on domestic politics. Unlike Tirpitz, he thought the conservative and bourgeois parties would refuse to increase the burden on taxpayers before the forthcoming general election for fear of losing ground to the social-democratic and left-liberal parties.

While other naval agencies, though sometimes only very reluctantly, supported Tirpitz, the Chancellor was able to mobilize the army against the navy. The army, which had been satisfied with its minor role in the past, now began to demand more money for an increase of its strength and equipment in order to meet the danger of a great war on the continent. A continental war seemed much more likely now than it had been for many years in the recent past. With the deteriorating position of the German Empire in Europe, and the failure of Tirpitz's plan, the importance of sea power was being questioned openly now.

In his struggle with the Chancellor he continued to argue that sea power was the foundation of world power. However, in 1909, he and the Chief of the Admiralty Staff admitted, "our chances in a war against England are not good under the present conditions."[64] Tirpitz began to feel desperate as his life's work fell to ruins. Competing with the army was difficult, almost useless. While support for a Navy Law in the *Reichstag* was lukewarm, its supporters pushed the army forward. "What safeguards our peace is not flexibility, agreements [and] understandings, but only our good German sword and the feeling that we are hoping to look up towards a government which will not allow this sword to rust when the appropriate time has come,"[65] the leader of the conservative party exclaimed in the *Reichstag* in early November.

The Kaiser and Tirpitz's closest collaborators began to waver in their support, for the Chancellor's argument for a new army bill and his reference to the political difficulties seemed convincing. The Kaiser agreed to the Chancellor's proposal to postpone the introduction of both a navy and an army law before the elections, giving the Chancellor time to thwart Tirpitz's plans.

For Tirpitz, this development meant he had to accept that the army was again to receive priority over the navy even though he still hoped that this decision would not fundamentally affect the realization of his naval program. In late December 1911, he gave up his demand of six new ships, asking for only three new ones on January 25, 1912, the day of the general elections, which returned the Social Democratic Party as the strongest party in the *Reichstag*. With three new ships he could still achieve a powerful fleet that Britain could not out-build in the long run.

On February 7, 1912, during the opening ceremony of the newly elected *Reichstag*, the Kaiser announced a new navy and army bill. However, Tirpitz's hope that he had been successful proved wrong. On February 8, 1912, Lord Haldane, the British Secretary of War, arrived in Berlin to negotiate an Anglo-German agreement. Tirpitz had been informed about this visit only a few days in advance. Haldane's visit was the result of a private initiative of a British banker, Sir Ernest Cassell, and the director of one of Germany's biggest shipping companies, Albert Ballin. Worried by rumors about the introduction of a new navy bill that could only result in a further deterioration of Anglo-German relations, they had paved the way for this visit. The British government, under pressure from its own radicals, was willing to improve its relations with Germany. Leading circles in Britain had realized that it was necessary to take a more conciliatory attitude towards Germany in order to avoid an explosion. They were willing to support "German colonial expansion on a large scale without damaging her own vital interests." There was only one condition: no new navy bill.[66] This offer seemed to open a way out of a political dilemma, for Britain was obviously willing to enter into negotiations again. Though both governments were aware of the restrictions on their freedom of maneuver, they had secular interest in exploring the possibility of an arrangement.

For Tirpitz, this sudden turn of events created a difficult situation. As he later wrote: "If we [...] invited the English to Berlin we had to be prepared to sacrifice something so as not to burden ourselves with the new embarrassment of a fruitless request. Bethmann's disinclination to represent the Bill before the *Reichstag* revealed to the English the point on which they could browbeat us, perhaps disconcert us in the building of our fleet, and at the same time widen the split the Government."[67] While the Chancellor wanted to improve Anglo-German relations by reaching an agreement which, in turn, "would with one blow change the political situation in Europe in our favour,"[68] he himself had nothing more to offer, when he entered into direct negotiations with a representative of the British government on February 9, 1912 for the first time. Though Tirpitz and Haldane wanted to improve Anglo-German relations, no compromise was reached in naval matters. While Haldane insisted that in return for colonial concessions "fundamental modification [of the Navy Law] was essential,"[69] Tirpitz only offered to leave open the date of the third new ship he had demanded in the *Novelle*. In his eyes that was all he could offer "in return for little gifts, which took the form of problematical colonies."[70]

Nevertheless, Tirpitz did not feel good about the conversation. Surprised by Britain's willingness to make concessions in the colonial field, one of his closest collaborators, Admiral Edvard Capelle, suggested dropping the *Novelle*. "Such an agreement is a success of our naval policy upon which the State Secretary could be prouder than on the passage of the *Novelle* which had been put forward under completely different circumstances and which had been reduced to a *torso* in the meantime," he argued.[71]

Tirpitz hesitated, afraid the public might accuse him of being too weak or of thwarting Germany's prospect of a large colonial empire in Africa.[72] In the end, he decided to stick to the *Novelle*, but he still had a long way to go to get it passed by the *Reichstag*. For many weeks the Chancellor who wanted to come to an agreement with the British cabinet put severe pressure upon Tirpitz. Eventually these attempts became a "vicious circle" and led to nothing. Whereas Bethmann Hollweg wanted Britain to sign a treaty in which it pledged "benevolent neutrality [...] if either of the high contracting parties becomes entangled in a war with one or more other Powers," the liberal cabinet was only willing to give vague promises that did not endanger Britain's relations with France and Russia.[73] When the Admiralty had pointed out that the increase of the fighting strength of the German navy and not the demand for three more ships was the most dangerous aspect of the new supplementary bill, the *Novelle* again stood in the way of an agreement. "The proposed new Fleet Law went a great way farther than was necessary for merely providing such a squadron as would relieve the active squadrons of the High Seas Fleet of Germany from the duty of training recruits,"[74] the British Foreign Secretary, Sir Edward Grey, told the German ambassador in late February.

On April 15, after heavy infighting, the *Novelle* was introduced into the *Reichstag* together with an army bill. On paper, Tirpitz had reached his aim. According to this law, the German Navy would have a formidable sea force of 41 battleships, 20 battle cruisers, 40 light cruisers, 144 torpedo boats, and 72 submarines. The Kaiser awarded him a higher class of Prussia's most important decoration, the Order of the Black Eagle, after the Novelle had passed the *Reichstag* smoothly in late May. At the same time, as though the Kaiser thus wanted to emphasize that Tirpitz's political strategy had proved right, one of the latter's most important adversaries in the struggle of how to deal with Britain, Count

Metternich, the German ambassador in London, was replaced by an obvious hard-liner.

In spite of this success the future looked bleak. Tirpitz soon had to realize that the financial constraints of this Navy Law would make further requests for naval increases impossible. Any technical innovation regarding either speed or gun-calibers would be difficult to follow for lack of money. Tirpitz was aware of these difficulties and continued to be haunted by the fear that his life's work might prove a failure in spite of the success he had just achieved. Disappointments, setbacks, and frustrations contributed to this state of mind. Tirpitz, who had been promoted to the rank of Grand Admiral in 1911, often felt isolated, misunderstood, and lonely. On many occasions he thought of resigning from the office he had held so successfully in the past. Despite many disappointments, he also still enjoyed his beer parties, *Bierabende*, with his officers and occasionally the Kaiser. He liked to talk freely with some of his younger officers and he visited the High Seas Fleet at anchor or took part in the great imperial maneuvers, *Kaisermanöver*, each spring or fall.

However, several incidents contributed to his increasing uneasiness and mistrust towards almost everybody, including the Kaiser. Though Admiral Holtzendorff, Commander-in-Chief of the High Seas Fleet, retired in 1913, relations between Tirpitz and the front did not improve. The front continued to complain about Tirpitz's neglect of its more immediate needs. He was soon convinced that neither Admiral Friedrich von Ingenohl, Holtzendorff's successor, nor Admiral Hugo von Pohl, who had succeeded Admiral August von Heeringen as Chief of the Admiral Staff, were capable of fulfilling the tasks they had taken over. Moreover, the events surrounding the introduction of the *Novelle* in 1912 had proven that he could not rely on Admiral von Müller, the influential Chief of the Naval Cabinet who had tried to pave the way for a compromise between Tirpitz and the Chancellor instead of fully backing Tirpitz alone. Most important was the fact that the Kaiser was obviously losing his interest in the navy and Tirpitz's policy. He often accused Tirpitz of making wrong decisions in technical matters or of building the wrong type of battleship. To Tirpitz's embarrassment, the Kaiser also showed an increasing lack of interest in his proposals and in his political advice. At the height of the Balkan crisis in 1912, the Kaiser ordered Tirpitz to prepare a new *Novelle*, only to drop it less than three weeks later in favor of a larger army bill, again confirming the priority of the army over the navy.[75] In the fall of 1913, Tirpitz travelled all the way from the Black Forest to the Kaiser's hunting lodge in East Prussia on the Russian border to discuss the naval estimates for 1914 with the Kaiser. He had just started to give his report when an aide-de-camp reported to the Kaiser that a big stag had been sighted. The Kaiser left the room without a word instead of listening to the State Secretary. Moreover, he still could not help feeling that the navy was only a mechanical toy for the Kaiser. He had the impression that the Kaiser held him responsible for Germany's bad relationship with Great Britain, the country of his mother and the idol he wanted to imitate in many respects. Though deeply hurt by this development in his relationship with the Kaiser, Tirpitz stayed in order to save his life's work

The course of domestic politics was also disappointing for Tirpitz. He thought the Chancellor was weak, unable to stem the "red flood" which threatened the existing order. He was convinced that Germany was "on the slide downwards,"[76] as he wrote in 1913. In spite of these bleak prospects, he was unwilling to attack the Chancellor, oust him out of office, and replace him as many conservatives openly demanded in the press. He argued that he was too old, but it seems more likely that he was not sure he would succeed. Appointing Tirpitz as Chancellor was similar to a declaration of war against Great Britain and although the Kaiser had always supported him, Tirpitz could not be sure of his confidence in this respect.

The development of the Royal Navy and Anglo-German relations remained a matter of great concern to Tirpitz. Britain had accepted the *Novelle* and not regarded it as an excuse to *Copenhagen* the High Seas Fleet as some had expected. Instead, Anglo-German relations seemed to improve, and during the Balkan crisis of 1912–13, both nations worked together to reach a peaceful settlement and avoid a European conflagration.

In his *Memoirs* Tirpitz argued that this change was the result of a new policy towards Great Britain, embodied by the new German ambassador to the Court of St. James, Baron Adoy Marschall von

Bieberstein: "His appearance in London […] put a stop for a time to the German method of kow-towing to the English and being impressed by their ways. Marschall knew that the Briton becomes more respectful, the more resolutely his competitor maintains his own standpoint. He declared that Germany could not carry out her economic policy without possessing a power at sea which could protect us against the necessity of yielding to England at every turn." His refusal to make concessions had proven right and paved the way for a more realistic policy towards Great Britain.

It is difficult to accept this interpretation of the development of Anglo-German relations on the eve of war. Tirpitz deliberately disregarded the fact that both British and German politicians had not discussed the naval question further in order to avoid future navy scares and their dangerous impact on foreign policy in both countries. Instead, they tried to ease tensions by solving minor questions like the future of the Portuguese colonies or the Baghdad Railway. When Churchill proposed "naval holidays" in 1913–14 or a visit to Germany to discuss the naval question with the Kaiser and Tirpitz, both governments anxiously tried to avoid any misunderstandings.

Tirpitz regarded this development of Anglo-German relations with great suspicion, afraid the Chancellor might sacrifice the navy for vague promises or useless territorial gains in Africa. Churchill's proposals of a fixed ratio of 16:10, which he only reluctantly accepted without wanting to sign an agreement, further strengthened his fear that politicians might waste what he had built up. In a secret speech to the officers of the Imperial Navy Office in October 1913, he summarized his political convictions: "Generally speaking the question whether Germany should fight for its place in the world against England […] or whether it should be content with the status of a second-rate power on the continent is a question of ones political faith. For a great nation, it seems more honourable to fight for the most important aim and to go under honourably instead of renouncing on a future without glory."[77]

All his rhetoric could not disguise the fact that he had lost the race against Germany's "most important enemy" in 1913–14. Whereas Churchill could later rightly proudly claim that "we were proceeding inflexibly for the third year in succession with our series of programmes according to scale and declaration," [78] Tirpitz and the navy still were not ready, as he had to admit in the infamous War Council of December 1912.[79] Moreover, the navy suffered from enormous financial problems. Since 1906 the cost of battleships rose from 36.8 to 57.5 million marks and the cost of battle cruisers rose from 27.7 to 46.6 million marks. Britain's decision to build Super-Dreadnoughts of the *Queen Elizabeth* class in 1912 showed that the Royal Navy would defend its superiority at all costs. Since any further increases in gun calibers, armor, and speed would help widen the gap between British and German ships, the Kaiser and Tirpitz were relieved to hear that the Royal Navy might reduce the caliber of the big guns of the new battleships. Though the Kaiser misjudged the situation when he concluded that this was "the first victory we have won over the British without firing any shot,"[80] he and Tirpitz had been worried. This was a new mindset; just the year before the Kaiser had been confident of winning the race against Great Britain, claiming: "We have them up against the wall," following Lord Haldane's mission to Berlin.[81]

In May 1914, Tirpitz wrote: "The situation collapses over the navy,"[82] and a few days later, he added: "We cannot build the ships anymore which we have planned."[853] Contrary to everything he had maintained before, Tirpitz now admitted defeat. He tried to develop new ideas of naval warfare and pressed for more money, but the Chancellor rejected his demands outright, and the Kaiser was lukewarm in his support.[84] Even Tirpitz did not have a clear idea of naval policy in the future and its role in a war with Great Britain. Neither Tirpitz nor anyone else seemed to know what would happen if the British did not come. Geography, which Tirpitz had always neglected when planning his fleet, now turned out to be a serious disadvantage. He toyed with the idea of building up a "flying" double-squadron of fast battle cruisers, which was supposed to wage cruiser-warfare in the Atlantic Ocean, but he postponed the discussion of this important change in naval strategy to a later date.[85]

On the eve of war, Tirpitz was prepared to fight for his plan once again, despite the growing difficulties. As Captain Albert Hopman noted in his diary with regard to the disputed supplementary budget in June 1914: "The nation and the *Reichstag* can't do anything else without damaging our national prestige severely."[86] The war, which broke out only weeks later, however, changed the situation completely.

Tirpitz was not directly involved in the events and decisions leading to the outbreak of war. He had gone on holiday in early July, only to be kept informed by his deputy in short daily reports. Accordingly he had no idea of the plans and political calculations of the Chancellor. When he returned against the wishes of the Chancellor he did not advise moderation for fear of a diplomatic defeat as in 1911. Though Tirpitz did not want war, he was willing to take great risks to avoid another defeat. Until July 30, he did not reckon with British intervention; in his eyes, Grey was only bluffing.[87] It soon became clear that the British Foreign Secretary was not bluffing. Though Tirpitz took part in many of the conferences between the Kaiser, the Chancellor, the Prussian Minister of War, and the Chief of the General Staff, they did not want his advice. The Chancellor did not, as Tirpitz feared he would, make a last minute agreement with Britain at the cost of the navy, but in the eyes of some decision-makers, it was responsible for the disaster of July 1914. "If you had only brought us a little naval agreement with England, the war would not have been necessary," the Secretary for Foreign Affairs Gottlieb von Jagow told Tirpitz on August 6.[88]

Tirpitz tried unsuccessfully to save his life's work. Concerning war with Britain, the navy did not have a definite war plan. It stayed on the defensive, trying to "damage the English through the guard and blockade forces in the German Bight by a mine and U-boat offensive extending to the British coast." Only after the "power relationship has been evened through such waging of war and the English forces have been weakened [...] it is to be attempted under favourable circumstances to engage our fleet in battle through the preparation and involvement of all its strength."[89] This was not a war according to the teachings of Mahan, and Tirpitz felt unhappy with it.

Moreover, right from the beginning of the war Tirpitz was convinced that Britain was responsible for the disasters that lay ahead. He later argued that "the old pirate State, England has again succeeded in letting Europe tear itself to pieces, and by throwing in her own power and applying the most brutal methods, she has secured a victory which accords with her material interests."[90] "The causa remota of the world-war" he continued, was less the government's lack in foreign politics but "the English policy of encirclement which originated in the 'nineties in trade jealousy, then hid behind pretexts (Transvaal, Navy) poisoned the press of the world, linked up all the anti-German forces in the world, and created a tense atmosphere in which the slightest mistake might cause a most terrible explosion."[91]

Tirpitz wrongly believed this interpretation of past events for the rest of his life. As Paul Kennedy has rightly argued: "It was [...] a blatant misinterpretation of past events for Tirpitz [...] to claim that the naval race had played no part in the causes of the First World War. As Bülow privately pointed out to him, even if Germany 'was dragged into the war through our clumsy handling of a Balkan problem [...] there is the question whether France and particularly Russia would have let it come to war had public opinion in England not been so greatly enraged precisely at the concentration of our great ships.'"[92]

Failure

Since being appointed Secretary of State for the Navy, Tirpitz had claimed that "his" navy was built either to deter war or to inflict heavy losses on its enemy, which would then be helpless towards its other rivals in the event of another war. He had even argued the High Seas Fleet might have a chance of winning a decisive battle. Tirpitz hoped that the High Seas Fleet would be able to do its duty as he had always promised, but this was not the case. The navy failed in challenging the Grand Fleet, breaking the distant blockade, and paving the way to world power.

The fear of complete failure haunted Tirpitz right from the outbreak of war. In late September 1914, Tirpitz wrote to his wife: "I shall tender my resignation immediately after the war. The reconstruction of the navy, if it ever comes to that, must be undertaken by someone else. Pohl, Müller, the Chancellor, and the Kaiser have kept back the fleet. I believe now that they won't fire a single gun, and the work of my life ends in less than nothing."[1]

On August 16, Tirpitz left Berlin for Coblenz in the Rhine valley with the Kaiser and the members of the Great Headquarters. Following the march of German troops into France, Belgium, and Luxembourg as closely as possible, the Kaiser and his entourage intended to direct events on the battlefields.

Whether his presence in the center of command would enable Tirpitz to exert influence on the course of German politics during the war in general or naval politics and strategy in particular was an open question.

Tirpitz and the navy had found themselves in a difficult position. In the first three weeks, the navy lost four small cruisers in the Baltic and North Sea. Covering a mine-laying operation off the Finnish Coast, the Light Cruiser *Magdeburg* had run aground in shallow waters and the Russian Navy was able to salvage the naval cipher book, which they passed onto the Royal Navy who could then read German naval messages and direct its operations accordingly. Four days later, British battle cruisers attacked German light forces. This attack displayed the strategic dilemma of the High Seas Fleet. First, the navy had been unable both to detect the attack early enough and to assemble a counter force. Second, the High Seas Fleet did not risk attacking the Grand Fleet in the open North Sea. Third, the heavy fighting which followed after this battle laid bare the difficulties in naval decision making.

This battle was a shock to Tirpitz for two reasons. Until he received a telegram telling him otherwise, Tirpitz was afraid that his eldest son, second lieutenant on the Light Cruiser *Mainz,* had gone down with the ship. He also felt deeply distressed. "If things go on like this," he wrote to his wife, our light forces will "soon be wiped out. The English will enclose us in a great circle of mines; then our fleet will be 'bottled.'"

Tirpitz dreaded the scenario of the army winning the war while the navy remained passive or suffered heavy losses. Against the background of Tirpitz's promises and the expectations of the public, the result of such an outcome would be unsatisfactory in many respects. First, Germany would remain a continental power instead of achieving world power status and becoming an equal partner of the British Empire in world politics. Second, without victory over Britain in a final encounter at sea, "perfidious Albion,"[2] would never make any concessions to Germany. Third, a passive role of the navy in a war won by the army alone would once gain give rise to demands to stop naval funding.

Tirpitz correctly claimed that the Chancellor and the Kaiser advocated a fleet-in-being-strategy when war broke out. The existence of the fleet should deter Britain from either attacking the German coast or landing expeditionary forces in the back of the German army. Whereas the Kaiser did not want to risk his ships, the Chancellor hoped that he could thus restrain Britain's war effort or make it easier for the British government to reach a compromise peace. If Britain would accept German hegemony on the continent, Germany would concede not to imperil Britain's status as the supreme world power. From a political point of view this was absurd, for the Chancellor once again ignored the principles of British policy. However, from a military point of view, this concept was not unreasonable. A fleet-in-being protected the German coasts and might be an important asset at peace negotiations, whereas a fleet, which was risked and lost in one decisive battle, could not be rebuilt quickly during the war.

Since 1897 Tirpitz had pursued a different political and naval strategy. In his eyes, only world power status could guarantee Germany's survival in the twentieth century. He wrote to his wife. "I have guaranteed that Germany should have a place in the world. For this she was bound to have a fleet. To build this fleet takes a long time, but it is now in a considerable measure ready, so that it should be able to take part in a world-war. [...] Many have counted on me, and I can't alter things, and the little that I could have done for the navy has been forbidden because they didn't want to lose their toy. For like everything else, it was only a toy."[3] From this perspective, the Chancellor, his supporters and the Kaiser were carelessly risking Germany's future. "Bethmann has merely continental conceptions. He doesn't see that we can no longer exist as a purely European continental State,"[4] he wrote as early as August 20, 1914, after a long conversation with the Chancellor in the Imperial Headquarters.

When war was declared, the decentralized command structure of the navy proved a serious impediment to Tirpitz's ambitions of further directing naval policy, strategy, and operations. In wartime, he was not the most important officer within the naval hierarchy. Now the Chief of the Naval Staff—the *Admiralstab*—Admiral von Pohl, became the chief adviser to the Kaiser. To Tirpitz's further dismay, the Chief of the Naval Cabinet, Admiral von Müller, was the most important link between the Kaiser and the chiefs of the different naval organizations, the navy, and the government. Tirpitz had hoped that the Kaiser would appoint him supreme commander of the navy, thus reviving the position that had been abolished at his own request in 1899. The Kaiser, who wanted to be his own supreme commander, refused and was only willing to assign a special role to Tirpitz at the outbreak of war. Owing to the deficiencies of Admiral von Pohl, who was generally regarded as a weak leader, Tirpitz was ordered to advise on operational matters on July 30. This decision soon proved the root of serious rivalries.

After August 28, 1914, Tirpitz had demanded a more offensive role of the High Seas Fleet. "The North Sea fleet," he wrote, "should create by continual activity a situation that would compel the English to draw nearer to us. If a battle developed in this manner on our initiative, not too far from our home waters, there was a possibility, especially in the earlier parts of the war, that the English would not throw the whole of their united forces into the fight."[5] However, the Kaiser wanted the Commander-in-Chief of the High Seas Fleet to be more cautious and not to risk the fleet through premature losses.[6]

Tirpitz later wrote that the first months of the war had a golden opportunity, which had been missed carelessly. When war broke out, the British margin of superiority over the High Seas Fleet was considerable but the strength of the Royal Navy in its most important theatre of war was dwindling away quickly. Newly commissioned ships were not fully efficient and others needed repair. Moreover, the Commander-in-Chief of the Grand Fleet, Admiral John Jellicoe, faced new challenges at the same time. In October 1914, the battleship *Audacious* sank in the Irish Sea after hitting a mine laid by a German auxiliary cruiser in the weeks before. In November, the German Cruiser Squadron heading for the German Bight from the South Seas defeated a British squadron under Admiral Christopher Craddock off the coast of Chile; at the same time Turkey entered the war on the side of the Central Powers. As a result five modern battle cruisers had to be dispatched to the South Atlantic and the Caribbean or had to stay in the Mediterranean to meet these threats against Britain's naval supremacy on the oceans. If the High Seas Fleet ever had a chance against the Grand Fleet in a major naval encounter, it was in the early months of the war.

Tirpitz realized that the High Seas Fleet might find itself in an awkward situation, if "the British did not come" as Admiral Heeringen had

Tirpitz and his brother, Max, 1950s. Tirpitz papers, courtesy of Deutsche Schiffahrtsmuseum Bremerhaven

Tirpitz as a young man, late 1860s. Tirpitz papers, courtesy of
Deutsche Schiffahrtsmuseum Bremerhaven

Tirpitz in 1883. Tirpitz papers, courtesy of Deutsche
Schiffahrtsmuseum Bremerhaven

Tirpitz and his wife Marie, 1880s. Tirpitz papers, courtesy of
Deutsche Schiffahrtsmuseum Bremerhaven

Tirpitz around 1890, as captain of the armored frigate SMS Preussen, *during a cruise in the Mediterranean.* Tirpitz papers, courtesy of Deutsche Schiffahrtsmuseum Bremerhaven

The German High Seas Fleet during maneuvers, before 1914.
Courtesy of the Deutsche Marinemuseum Wilhelmshaven

*Tirpitz and the Emperor during a deer hunt in
Eastern Prussia, 1899.* Author's collection

Tirpitz in the uniform of a Grand Admiral, 1911.
Author's collection

Tirpitz as a member of the Order of the Black Eagle, Prussia's highest order. Tirpitz papers, courtesy of Deutsche Schiffahrtsmuseum Bremerhaven

Tirpitz in the uniform of a Grand Admiral. Tirpitz papers, courtesy of Deutsche Schiffahrtsmuseum Bremerhaven

The German Emperor, Wilhelm II, Tirpitz, and the Chief of the Prussian General Staff, Colonel General Helmuth von Moltke the Younger on board a German battleship on January 1, 1913. Tirpitz papers, courtesy of Deutsche Schiffahrtsmuseum Bremerhaven

The German High Seas Fleet during a raid against the British Coast, 1914. Courtesy of the Deutsche Marinemuseum Wilhemshaven

Tirpitz and Field Marshall Paul von Hindenburg in East Prussia, 1915. Tirpitz papers, courtesy of Deutsche Schiffahrtsmuseum Bremerhaven

Tirpitz and his wife Marie in front of their house in Feldafing on Lake Starnberg, 1926. Tirpitz papers, courtesy of Deutsche Schiffahrtsmuseum Bremerhaven

Tirpitz as a deputy of the Reichstag *in his office in parliament, 1927.* Tirpitz papers, courtesy of Deutsche Schiffahrtsmuseum Bremerhaven

Tirpitz and members of his family during the official celebration of his 80th birthday, 1929. Tirpitz papers, courtesy of Deutsche Schiffahrtsmuseum Bremerhaven

Vice Admiral Schmidt congratulating Tirpitz on his 80th birthday in 1929. Tirpitz papers, courtesy of Deutsche Schiffahrtsmuseum Bremerhaven

Tirpitz's house in Feldafing on Lake Starnberg. Tirpitz papers, courtesy of Deutsche Schiffahrtsmuseum Bremerhaven

Tirpitz's funeral in Munich, March 1930. Tirpitz papers, courtesy of Deutsche Schiffahrtsmuseum Bremerhaven

Tirpitz's tomb in Munich, 1930. Tirpitz papers, courtesy of Deutsche Schiffahrtsmuseum Bremerhaven

The German Battleship Tirpitz *during World War II.*
Courtesy of the Deutsche Marinemuseum Wilhemshaven

Wählt Großadmiral von Tirpitz
den Kandidaten
der Deutsch-nationalen Volkspartei!

Propoganda postcard for Tirpitz's election campaign in 1924: "Vote for Tirpitz, the candidate of the Deutsch-nationale Volkspartei (German National People's Party). Author's collection

put it in 1912. But there is no evidence that he had an answer to this question. Though Germany was better off than Britain regarding naval bases in case a battle took place under the guns of Heligoland, he also had no idea of how to force the Grand Fleet to seek battle under conditions which were only favorable for the High Seas Fleet. In August, Tirpitz toyed with the idea of sending flying squadrons consisting of battle cruisers to attack Britain's lifelines. In September, after the unexpected success of U 9, which had sunk three British armored-cruisers within one hour, he thought he had opened up new perspectives in naval strategy. However, Tirpitz's enthusiasm for new ideas abated quickly, for in both cases, there is no evidence that the Secretary of State was willing to give up deep-seated convictions of naval warfare at least for the time being.

These convictions demanded a battle, but Tirpitz's attitude was ambivalent. He asked, is it true for "the greatest effort to be successful,"[7] and criticized the defensive strategy advocated by Pohl, Ingenohl and Müller. In late October, he repeated his pledge for an offensive strategy during a visit of the High Seas Fleet at Wilhelmshaven and Kiel and in November, demanded the establishment of a unified naval command under his leadership, all to no avail. His intention to outmaneuver his rivals within the navy and put his stamp on naval strategy was too obvious to be considered seriously. The Chief of the Imperial Headquarters, General Hans von Plessen, told him that the Kaiser would not like to let him go, for he was too important as an adviser in both political and in naval affairs.[8] This was nothing but a polite rejection of his attempts to interfere with the prerogatives of the Kaiser in naval affairs.

Contrary to his later allegations, there is enough evidence to suggest that Tirpitz, too, was willing to risk a battle *only* if the Grand Fleet appeared roughly one hundred or even less nautical miles off Heligoland.[9] In mid-August he warned of seeking the enemy and advised strikes against the entrance into the Channel and the Thames estuary to whittle down the strength of the Grand Fleet. On August 19, he justified the defensive role of the navy to the Chief of the Military Cabinet, General Moriz von Lyncker. In his diary, Lyncker wrote: "From a military point of view this attitude is justified. I also believe that it is desirable to possess at least a part of the fleet in future peace negotiations."[10] In October, Tirpitz wrote to Admiral Ingenohl that he was now convinced a battle was very unlikely. Nevertheless, he still asked for an offensive strike for reasons of naval prestige. At the same time he once again assured Ingenohl of his confidence into his abilities as commander-in-chief of the High Seas Fleet, only to change his mind a few days later and to demand the latter's replacement with the Chief of the Naval Staff, Admiral Pohl.

Tirpitz's attempts in the 1920s to create the impression that his statements and suggestions in favor of an offensive role of the High Seas Fleet had always been consistent and that a decisive battle had been the ultimate aim of his endeavors are not convincing. During and after the war, Tirpitz's prestige was great enough to stifle his critics. The official naval history, the *Seekriegswerk*, supported his interpretation of the past. In the late 1920s, Vice-Admiral Eberhard von Mantey, the director of the German naval archives, admitted that this interpretation was neither justified nor a fair judgement of Ingenohl's behavior as Commander-in-Chief. It is striking that Mantey did not risk saying this in public for fear of being openly attacked by high-ranking former admirals who still defended their "master" against his critics with every available means.

Due to his contradictory behavior, Tirpitz's increasingly fierce critique of his opponents created the impression that his behavior was not motivated by a diverging conception of naval warfare but by his intention to preserve his own reputation which had begun to deteriorate very quickly due to the obvious uselessness of the navy.

This impression was correct, but it missed one important point. For Tirpitz the use of the battle fleet and the existence of a powerful navy after the war were inseparable. On August 30, 1914, he wrote to his wife: "Bethmann continually tried to influence Pohl not to coop up the fleet. That would be the death of our navy after the war. He and the whole bunch of diplomats want to sell the fleet at the conclusion of the peace with England, that is the whole secret."[11] In early October he wrote: "It is true the English fleet doesn't come out. I don't want to have our fleet start for England and fight there. But I do believe it to be absolutely wrong policy that Ingenohl should be given orders 'to risk nothing' against superior forces. That means, in other words, that our fleet is to be embalmed, and then imagine the peace!"[12] Tirpitz's frustration was further increased by the idea that the army would soon be victorious, while the navy would have to wait for another chance in the distant future.

Tirpitz's life in the Great Headquarters was difficult. He now played only a minor role in the entourage of the Kaiser and within the nation's political and military leadership. To Tirpitz's dismay the small number of naval officers in the Great Headquarters had to lodge in a separate house where they had very little direct contact with the army, the Chancellor, and the Kaiser. "I have a feeling that we are not wanted anywhere," he wrote to his wife.[13] Whereas the Chief of the General Staff reported to the Kaiser every morning, Tirpitz was invited only occasionally. Moreover, contact between the heads of the army and the navy was loose as well. Sometimes, operational matters and questions of grand strategy were discussed at lunch, but not during official meetings between the chiefs of staffs. Tirpitz's attitude to work behind the scenes and criticize almost everybody and every decision contributed to his isolation, which increased his discontent.

The reports of Tirpitz's close follower, Captain Hopman, about his conversations with Tirpitz during their long daily walks and Tirpitz's letters to his wife in Berlin give a vivid description of his frustration, anger, and desperate attempts to save his life's work. Tirpitz tried to find scapegoats to blame for the deficiencies of German naval policy, naval strategy, and politics in general. In Tirpitz's eyes, the Kaiser and his entourage were responsible for the disaster that would follow. They had carelessly led Germany into a war that they were unable to conduct successfully. In his desperation, Tirpitz even looked for authoritarian solutions to solve the problems underlying German politics and naval strategy. Now openly blaming the Kaiser for the failure of German world and naval politics, Tirpitz wanted to force him to abdicate in favor of the crown prince or to go on "sick leave" for a while. Though many of the generals he approached in spring 1915 also complained about the Kaiser's behavior, none of them were willing to support this scheme. Unlike Tirpitz, who was prepared to violate his oath of allegiance to the Kaiser for the sake of the nation and of the monarchy, they still regarded the monarch as untouchable. Tirpitz had no choice but to let the matter rest.

Tirpitz felt deeply frustrated by the development of the war at sea, but the situation of the navy was not as bleak as it seemed. On October 3, Pohl, Ingenohl, and the three commanders of the battle squadrons reaffirmed the decision to continue the defensive strategy. This decision was based on the assumption that it was more important to keep the navy intact than to risk a dangerous encounter with the Grand Fleet. This decision, however, did not preclude strikes against the British coast or offensive mine-laying operations in the North Sea. For reasons of morale, Ingenohl was anxious for such operations, and it would not take long until the High Seas Fleet embarked on bombarding the British East Coast. On November 3, German battle cruisers under Admiral Franz von Hippel shelled Great Yarmouth and Sunderland. On December 15–16 the whole High Seas Fleet fired on Hartlepool, Whitby, and Scarborough. On both occasions the German vessels returned safely. In January 1915 these strikes were given up after the loss of the armored cruiser *Blücher* during a raid against British fishing vessels. This raid proved a disaster, Ingenohl was accused of having sent out his cruisers without any support of the battle fleet and was replaced with the Chief of the Naval Staff only a few days later. The fact that Ingenohl had only followed the Kaiser's orders not to risk the fleet was ignored.

Since the December raid, Tirpitz had been convinced that Ingenohl was the wrong man in the important position he held because he "had the fate of Germany in the palm of his hands" and had let it slip away.[14] Reports by Captain Hopman confirmed that Ingenohl was regarded as a weak leader and that he had lost the confidence of his men.[15] Tirpitz hoped that he would now be able to direct the course of the naval war. This was not the case. Pohl had been replaced with Admiral Gustav Bachmann, the Chief of the Baltic naval station.

Tirpitz was surprised and angered by the declaration of unrestricted submarine warfare in the North Sea, which had been taken at Pohl's initiative at the beginning of February 1915. In a war zone around Great Britain and Ireland, including the Channel, every enemy merchantman found in that area would be destroyed. Though only British vessels were meant, it was likely that neutral ships would also be affected owing to the misuse of neutral flags ordered by the British government.[16]

Tirpitz did not object to this kind of warfare for principle reasons.

In an interview with an American journalist, he had mentioned submarine warfare as a possible answer to Britain's blockade. "If pressed to the utmost, why not," he had asked the journalist, obviously hoping to avoid hostile reactions from the U.S. government in the case of sinking neutral ships with American citizens on board. On January 25, 1915, Tirpitz sent an astonishing memo to the Chief of the Naval Cabinet. In a dramatic *volte de face* he admitted that successes against the Grand Fleet were unlikely. Instead, he called for airship attacks on London, cruiser warfare in the Atlantic, and submarine warfare against Britain's lifelines.[17] However, when submarine warfare was declared only a few days later, he was convinced that this step had been taken too early. So far, the number of submarines that could be effectively deployed against Great Britain was still too small. Only a third of the twenty-nine existing submarines were available. Many of these were outdated, and only fifteen new ones were expected to go into service in the months to come. Moreover, the navy still lacked the submarine bases and its commanders still had no experience in this kind of warfare. Pohl rejected these objections, arguing that the Chancellor, the Foreign Office, and the general staff had approved of his plan. The submarine seemed a perfect means to cut off Britain from its important supply lines. Eventually, Tirpitz also approved this strategy against Great Britain. "Within six weeks after the beginning of submarine warfare," Britain would give in, he even declared on February 16, 1915.[18] After the war, Tirpitz tried to play down this statement, which, for the first time, had announced that the navy was able to end the war within a fixed limit of time.

The corollary of Tirpitz's demand for an offensive against Britain was his demand for an annexation of Belgium, a common war aim among industrialists, politicians in the *Reichstag,* and many members of the government. Tirpitz, however, became one of the most ardent supporters of this idea. He emphasized the need of acquiring a naval base in Belgium, which was "a question of the greatest importance for the future of Germany." Such a naval base would decisively strengthen Germany's position towards Great Britain and force it to respect our position in the world."[19] Accordingly, the Belgian question became something of an *idée fixe* for him because he was afraid that the Chancellor and army generals seemed to prefer to extend the nation's borders in the east instead of the west. "Falkenhayn has told Bachmann [Chief of the Admiral Staff in 1915] that the Chancellor wants to annex Courland; the English will take pleasure in that, for then we shall sit tight, for a hundred years, and the Russians the same. Then England laughs in her sleeve; and we withdraw from Belgium. Then England will have gained her object, and we shall be reduced to a mere second-class continental State again."[20] Subsequently, he never gave up his demand for an annexation of Belgium, which he also regarded as justified as a means to maintain "our pre-war economic influence in Antwerp," to liberate "our kinsmen, the Flemings, from the foreign rule of Franco-Walloons," and, of course to remove the "English from the continental coast."[21]

The view of ending the war by reverting to completely new means of warfare soon proved carelessly optimistic. Tirpitz and supporters of submarine warfare within the navy underestimated the political problems, that this revision of strategy would entail. Though the Chancellor had given his consent to the declaration of the war-zone, he and the Foreign Office took great pains at avoiding any conflict with neutral countries, especially the United States. For weeks the navy, the Chancellor, and the Kaiser quarrelled about how to answer American protests against the declaration of the war-zone and whether there was a way to observe maritime law, which would alleviate neutral fears. In his *Memoirs*, Tirpitz wrote: "Before the campaign born on February 4th had drawn its first breath, its own parents were hurrying panic-stricken to throttle it."[22]

The navy deliberately underestimated the problems of unrestricted submarine warfare. On May 7, 1915, *U 20* torpedoed the British passenger liner *Lusitania,* killing 128 American citizens. In order to keep the United States out of the war, the Chancellor tried to restrict submarine warfare. When all submarine commanders were ordered not to sink large passenger-liners, a severe crisis followed. Spearheaded by Tirpitz, the navy regarded any surrender from the position taken up before as "a political defeat." "Sparing neutrals or compensating them for the sinking of their vessels actually encourages sailings to England under neutral flag," and "only the energetic conduct of the campaign can turn the insular position of England from advantage to disadvantage," the navy argued.[23]

In order to increase the pressure on the Chancellor and the Kaiser, Tirpitz and the Chief of the Naval Staff, Admiral Bachmann, handed in their resignations twice, June 6 and August 27, 1915. The Kaiser was outraged when he was informed of these reactions to his decisions. In his eyes this was an act of "felony" and a "military conspiracy initiated by Tirpitz," which he did not want to tolerate.[24] While Bachmann was replaced with Tirpitz's outspoken rival, Admiral Holtzendorff, Tirpitz was ordered to remain in office, though his functions were curtailed.

In September 1915, after renewed American protests against submarine warfare, following the sinking of the *Arabic* by *U 24* the month before, the navy was ordered "to suspend all submarine activities of any sort on west coast and in Channel, and to carry on in North Sea only in accordance with Prize Orders."[25]

This order was a deep blow to Tirpitz who had hoped to use the successes in the submarine campaign to bolster his reputation, which had suffered from the inactivity of the High Seas Fleet, and to increase his influence on German politics.

Though Tirpitz had to stay in the background for the time being, he found a new ally at the end of the year, the Chief of the General Staff, General Erich von Falkenhayn. Falkenhayn had never liked Tirpitz and was convinced that naval building had been a waste of money. However with the end of the war still out of sight, Falkenhayn decided to combine on the French stronghold at Verdun with a renewal of the submarine campaign. Admiral Holtzendorff had now also become convinced that only submarine warfare could help end the war. The longer the war lasted, the greater the risk that Germany would lose it and that the home front would collapse as a result of the British "hunger-blockade." Then, the whole monarchy and the old system would be in danger of being overturned by a social revolution. "Immediate and relentless recourse to the submarine weapon is absolutely necessary. Any further delay […] will give England time for further naval and economic defensive measures, cause us greater losses in the end, and endanger quick success. […] If we defeat England, we break the backbone of the hostile coalition," Tirpitz argued in February 1916.[26] Moreover, unlike 1915, the navy maintained that it now possessed enough submarines to be successful within six months. Even if the United States entered the war on Britain's side, they would not be able to send their troops to Europe before the war had ended.

Falkenhayn and Tirpitz underestimated the opposition of the Chancellor. Like in 1915, Bethmann Hollweg did not want to risk a conflict with the United States. As before, he tried to drag on inter-governmental discussions as long as possible. When one of Tirpitz's subordinates gave a wrong figure on the number of submarines built or being built, he ousted Tirpitz from office in March 1916. The Kaiser agreed with the Chancellor. Asked to put in his resignation, Tirpitz officially requested his dismissal on March 12, 1916. "I have served Your Majesty with all my strength in the advancement of Your Majesty's life-work of showing to the German people the way across the sea into the world," he wrote, but "in the decisive fight against the enemies who seek to bar us by the sword from this path of national development, Your Majesty has not been able to follow my advice."[27] This argument missed one important point: Tirpitz's advice had proved wrong. The Kaiser granted his request on March 15, 1916. An era ended.

Many members of the government were relieved that Tirpitz was gone, but his supporters were outraged.[28] In their eyes his dismissal indicated that the government was about to look for a compromise peace instead of fighting for victory. Telegrams and letters of support flooded his home, and in the *Reichstag*, rightists staged a fierce attack against the Chancellor. Censorship muted this outcry, but could not suppress it.

The influential leader of the National Liberal Party, Ernst Bassermann, compared Tirpitz's dismissal to that of Bismarck, Germany's "Iron Chancellor," in 1890, which had been a turning point in German history just as much as Tirpitz's dismissal would soon prove a similar decisive event in the history of the German empire. Such a comparison was far-fetched.

Despite Tirpitz's exhaustion, deep hurt and disappointment, he did not withdraw from politics after twenty years in office. He did refuse to spearhead the opposition against the Chancellor and the Kaiser as many of his supporters were expecting, but behind the scenes he began to intrigue against the government by continuing his fight for unrestricted submarine warfare. On June 1, 1916, the German High Seas Fleet won a great victory against the Grand Fleet which, in Tirpitz's eyes, not only vindicated his policy since 1897 but also his demand for offensive action during the war. The enormous amount of telegrams congratulating him on this victory showed once again that he and his life's work were highly esteemed by his former political allies and friends. His most ardent supporters were members of the "new right" movement who were dissatisfied with the course of the government. Its most important key-figure was Wolfgang Kapp, a government official in East Prussia and a member of the Conservative Party. Kapp liked to engage in populist agitation in order to propagate his goals. He had excellent links to leading generals and courtiers, industrialists and professors, the conservative press and party politicians. For Kapp, Tirpitz seemed to be the right man to help him achieve his goal of declaring unrestricted submarine warfare. For only victory could realize far-reaching annexations in the West and in the East, and the imposition of an authoritarian regime in Germany to stop the socialist tide.[29] Using his good relations, Kapp soon advocated replacing the Chancellor with Tirpitz. Previously, the Chancellor had always been able to rally enough support behind him, and the military situation had improved as a result of German victories in the East and in the Balkans so that there seemed to be no real need to replace him by a strong man, at least for the time being.

In 1916, however, the situation had completely changed. The German attack on Verdun that was supposed to let France "bleed white" had proved a failure. In August 1916, Romania entered the war, adding a new front to those that already existed. Moreover the impact of the blockade, which the High Seas Fleet had been unable to break, was felt increasingly stronger at home. As a result, public discontent was rising and the political truce, the *Burgfriede*, which had been concluded at the outbreak of war became more fragile every day. Against this darkening horizon, Tirpitz seemed the right man to help save Germany. "Once Tirpitz—along with Hindenburg stands next to our Kaiser again, the faith and strength of our people will be completely dedicated to the Kaiser until victory. I believe that Germany will then return to its proper path to a strong Kaiserdom,"[30] one of Tirpitz's followers wrote to a member of the Kaiser's entourage.

Attempts to make Tirpitz chancellor failed. In spite of the support he still enjoyed at court, the Kaiser harshly rebuffed this proposal in a way "that cut off all further discussion,"[31] Ludendorff remembered after the war. The Kaiser realized that appointing Tirpitz chancellor would not only undermine his own position, but also exacerbate political tensions at home due to his open advocacy of annexations and dictatorial government.

In 1917, Tirpitz stepped back into the open. Though he had not become chancellor, he and those who backed him had achieved one important victory. In February 1917, the government had declared unrestricted submarine warfare, fully aware that it risked the entry of the United States into the war that followed in April. However, after a year of stalemate, heavy losses and the fact that another year of war might have a disastrous impact on the population, the government had accepted the navy's claim that unrestricted submarine warfare was the only means of forcing Britain to its knees soon.

It was soon clear that this campaign would not achieve its aim. Moreover, food had been sparse in the last winter, *Hungerwinter*, and when the Czarist regime in Russia was overthrown in March, the demand of the Russian revolutionaries for a peace without annexations and reparations was soon shared by many Germans who now also urged for the introduction of those reforms which had been promised at the beginning of the war but which had not made much progress. Change seemed imminent. In April the Kaiser promised a reform of the much-hated Prussian suffrage, and in July a majority of the *Reichstag* passed a resolution demanding peace without annexations and reparations. Even though the importance of this resolution should not be overestimated since the new Chancellor, Georg Michaelis, who had replaced Bethmann Hollweg, had no intention to regard it as a basis of his policy, these developments seemed alarming in the eyes of the political right.

Tirpitz, despite his disappointment that his attempts to become chancellor himself had failed, now openly collaborated with Kapp and his friends to pressure the government and to encourage the people to sustain as well as to change the course of domestic politics. Though Tirpitz did not share Kapp's idea of stimulating a mass movement which raised him on a shield and made his appointment as chancellor inevitable, he agreed to the latter's plan to stiffen the home front and to block domestic reforms. On September 1, 1917, Tirpitz became chairman of the "German Fatherland Party." This party, which did not want to be a party in the literal sense of the word "was intrinsically rightist in that it sought to divert attention from domestic reform and to foster a bonapartist synthesis of military victory and popular military dictatorship."[32]

What did this mean for Tirpitz? For many, he did appear as savior at the very last moment. "It seemed as if, in the twelfth hour, a star had appeared galvanizing our last hope,"[33] a member of the Admiral Staff noted in his diary. Tirpitz entered the political with a passion for fighting. Drawing heavily on his prestige, he emphasized the importance of fighting England, but his attempt to appear neutral in domestic matters failed.

By the summer, Tirpitz began to realize that he had reached his limits. In general, he had only reached those who had always listened to him, but not the masses as he had hoped. Moreover, it had become clear to him that a rightist movement would have no chance of success in the near future.

As a result, he slowly pulled out of the party's activities, withdrawing to his house in the Black Forest. From there he watched the course of events, trying again several times behind the scenes to bring about a fundamental change at the last minute. "We must make an appeal to the whole people to defend with determination our honour and our future existence, and we must at the same time act at once, both at home and abroad, in such a manner as to leave not the least doubt of our determination,"[34] he appealed to the new Chancellor, Prince Max of Baden, on October 17, 1918. A second letter written on October 30 remained unanswered. His attempts to establish a military dictatorship proved futile. It was an irony of fate that the navy he had built up had already mutinied when he wrote this letter; within a few days the mutineers received increasing support from the masses who wanted peace and who had no confidence in the old system. His suggestions to use brute military force to subdue the revolutionary movement in the early days of November were also not followed. On November 9, 1918, the monarchy collapsed. While he had to go into hiding due to the widespread hatred of officers and the turmoil in the capital, his fleet was soon surrendered to the Grand Fleet which—in the eyes of many German naval officers—took it to Scapa Flow under dishonorable circumstances. As he had always feared since the beginning of the war, his life's work lay in ruins and the future was bleak.

Grey Excellence

Though Tirpitz withdrew to a friend's home in the countryside after the military defeat in order to avoid the revolutionary turmoil in Berlin, his political career was not over. In the loneliness of a small hunting lodge in Pomerania, he sat down to write his memoirs. Tirpitz had started collecting his private papers and copies of official naval documents early in his life. During his daily walks in the Imperial Head-quarters in 1914–15 he had also dictated his recollections of specific events in the past. However, he was very reluctant to write his memoirs after he had been dismissed in March 1916 even though many histori-ans urged him do so for political reasons. The collapse of the old mo-narchical order, the fate of "his" fleet, and the public attacks finally made him change his mind. He was one of the first members of the old regime to publish his memoirs in late 1919. He wanted to make clear that he was still willing to fight for his ideas, "upright and unbroken" as ever before, in spite of the dramatic changes that had occurred in the meantime. Tirpitz had always been sensitive to critique, and justifying his life's work was no doubt his driving motive.

"The German people," he concluded, "did not understand the sea. In the hour of its destiny it did not use its fleet. Today, all that I can do for the fleet is to write its epitaph. Our nation has passed through a tragedy without parallel in its swift rise to the position of a world-power and its still swifter decline, due to the temporary short-sightedness of its politics and its lack of national feeling."[1] These were strong words, which left no doubt that neither he nor the navy were to be blamed for what had happened before and during the Great War. "The collapse," he argued, "is not to be attributed to our old constitution itself, but to the incompetence of the men who administered it."[2] In his description of his life and of the development of the navy he went into detail. He castigated the Chancellor's policy towards Great Britain, his misman-agement of the July crisis, and Bethmann Hollweg's opposition against the introduction of unrestricted submarine-warfare before 1917. He also accused the Naval Cabinet of undermining "the spirit of the fleet,"[3] and blamed the Kaiser for his indecision, weakness, and inability to fulfill the duties of a supreme warlord.

Tirpitz's verdict about the past did not mean that he welcomed the change Germany had undergone since the outbreak of revolution. He said, "The old state was certainly in need of improvement in many re-spects, but it was fully capable of development to meet the new era and the needs of our children and our children's children. The revolution, however, the greatest crime against the future of our people, jettisoned everything that had made us mighty."[4] Subsequently, the new order seemed inadequate to solve the problems the nation was facing now, for, as he claimed, "the republican idea as it has developed in Germany rests on promises to the masses that cannot be carried out. The demo-crats are thus forced, in order to keep control of the masses, to put 'rights' into the foreground, leaving 'duty' in the rear. This way can never lead us upwards."[5] This deep-seated mistrust towards democracy and the masses was typical of many conservatives who had difficulty coping with change and were unwilling to accept responsibility for mili-tary defeat and the collapse of the monarchical order.

The reception of his direct and indirect critique of the old system and the Kaiser was mixed. In spite of the latter's shortcomings and Bethmann Hollweg's obvious mistakes, Tirpitz's accusation seemed det-rimental to the defense against the war-guilt charge and the monarchi-cal idea itself. In the eyes of the adherents of the former system, he undermined all hopes of a restoration of the monarchy in the near future. The Kaiser's brother, Prince Henry, who had recovered from the shock of revolutionary turmoil, was the first member of the old elites to reprimand Tirpitz for his disloyal behavior and his violation of the traditional naval code of honor in late 1919.[6]

Tirpitz remained firm in his convictions. To alleviate his critics, he tried to defend the monarchical system but continued to fight for his ideas. The Allies' demand to extradite Tirpitz and other war criminals was another opportunity for him to attack the existing order. The Treaty of Versailles had stipulated that all German war criminals were to be put on trial for crimes committed during the war. Tirpitz was accused of violating international law by waging unrestricted submarine warfare. While the government tried to find a compromise, Tirpitz hoped that this attempt to humiliate Germany would give rise to a mass movement. He and his son were willing to fight and to die with their guns in their hands in order to avoid arrest and extradition. Unfortunately for him, the government negotiated with the Allies instead of attacking them head-on.

These events did not discourage Tirpitz from giving advice to the members of a younger generation and supporting their schemes against the Weimar Republic, though not as an active politician but as a grey excellence.[7] Tirpitz began to rally the German right in late 1920. Though all right-wing groups and parties pretended to pursue similar political aims, their disunity and factional rivalry were notorious. Instead of fighting the common enemy, democrats and socialists alike, they often rivaled with each other.

The center of the German right-wing movement was the capital of Bavaria, Munich. While Prussia was governed by a coalition of social democrats and liberals, a conservative government had taken power. For more than a decade the Bavarian capital played a crucial role in the formation of right-wing groups and attempts to overthrow the government in Berlin. In Munich, these groups could freely meet and discuss their putschist plans. Former Quarter Master General, General Ludendorff, and Adolf Hitler soon played an important role on the political stage in Bavaria. Both had founded parties of their own and tried to rally members of all classes behind new ideologies that said taking revenge for the "Dictate of Versailles," would make Germany a powerful nation again.

In late 1922, Tirpitz was invited to a conference on "National Propaganda in the Countryside" in Munich to discuss the best strategy to overcome the existing order. This invitation and Tirpitz's journey to Munich were the beginning of his relationship with the center of the German right which was to last until the end of his life.

Deeply committed to national revival, Tirpitz tried to form an alliance among right-wing parties and organizations, and the leadership of the army, the *Reichswehr*. This alliance aimed at overthrowing the government at Berlin. He did not want to putsch openly against the government. Instead, he thought of combining illegal and legal means. Tirpitz was convinced that a propaganda campaign similar to those he had inaugurated before would be the best means to great success. In a letter to former General Erich Ludendorff, Tirpitz wrote in December: "Without doubt, the right thing to do is to stir up hatred against France all over. If we succeed, we will indirectly strengthen national feeling among the working masses and drive back their sympathies for international movements."[8] Tirpitz hoped to induce the people to call for a national dictatorship headed by a leading Bavarian right-wing politician, Gustav von Kahr, to achieve his aims. These aims remained vague. In domestic politics Tirpitz thought of reintroducing the Bismarckian constitution to strengthen the authority of a strong government and reduce the influence of the parties in the *Reichstag*. In foreign policy, a restoration of Germany's national prestige and status as a great power in the world were the main points on his political agenda.

In hindsight, Tirpitz's plans appear unrealistic and amateurish. However, in 1922–23 against the background of an increasing chaos, things looked different. Tirpitz reckoned with the support of men like Hugo Stinnes, Adolf Hitler, General Ludendorff, their respective followers, and Georg Escherich, the organizer of home guards. Tirpitz believed that the course of events would vindicate his strategy. To some extent, his ideas were shared by many contemporaries who were disappointed by continual party-strife and the humiliating attitude of the Allies towards Germany. In mid-November 1922, the government of Chancellor Joseph Wirth had collapsed and the parties in the *Reichstag* proved unable to form a new coalition. In the meantime, political extremists from the right and left had intensified their attacks on the Weimar Republic. Sharp divisions among the political and social classes, separatist movements, and political violence on the streets as well as against prominent republicans were alarming signs of the deteriorating situation in Germany. In 1922, inflation had begun to gallop, indicating that Weimar's economy was also on the verge of collapsing in the near future. Finally, since the Genoa conference on reparations in May 1922, tensions with France about this issue had steadily risen and in January 1923, Paris sent troops into the Ruhr area to enforce its claims emanating from the Treaty of Versailles by confiscating coal and other goods. Only a strong authoritarian government seemed able to overcome these difficulties and setbacks on the way back to political normalcy and economic recovery. In late 1923, when the political and economic crisis culminated in diverse uprisings, even President Friedrich Ebert, a social democrat, seems to have played with the idea of establishing a dictatorship. However, where he wanted to save democracy, Tirpitz and his political allies intended to destroy it once and forever.

Tirpitz still refused to openly start a new political career, but he closely watched the development of the political situation in 1923, hoping that the Ruhr struggle and rising tensions at home and with France would reach such a point that the establishment of a nationalist dictatorship in Berlin was possible. He promoted this idea in his talks with leading representatives of the old elites. In order to unite the political right as well as to alleviate separatist moods in Bavaria, he even traveled to Munich to mediate a compromise between rivaling groups in mid-1923. At this occasion he also met Hitler for the first time. Unlike many others around him, Tirpitz did not like him. After the meeting he noted: "This man may have a noble turn of mind; to me he seems inaccessible to arguments: a fanatic inclined to craziness whom pampering has made unrestrained."[9] Though Tirpitz had occasionally played with the idea of using Hitler's demagogic talents in order to rally the scattered right, he resented his hatred of Jews and doubted his talents as a statesman. Tirpitz was still convinced that only a traditional and widely respected conservative like Kahr and not a young man like Hitler would be able to take the lead in the expected struggle for the formation of a national dictatorship. Tirpitz underestimated Hitler. While Tirpitz was trying to find a basis for a nationalist dictatorship in Berlin, Hitler and Ludendorff refused to wait. They wanted to exploit the political and economic crisis that seemed more favorable than ever before: A conflict between the governments in Berlin and Munich about the role of the Bavarian *Reichswehr* command, which had openly disobeyed orders to forbid further publication of the newspaper of Hitler's party, had quickly escalated. Relieved of his command, the commanding general of *Reichswehr* troops in Bavaria, General Otto von Lossow, had put himself under Kahr's command. Unwillingly, he nourished the notion that they might be willing to support Hitler and his followers in their attempt to overthrow the government at Berlin from Munich. On November 8, Hitler and Ludendorff started a putsch by storming the Beer Hall where Kahr was giving a speech and marching to the Feldherrnhalle in Munich the next day. Their attempt to imitate the example of the Italian Fascist leader Benito Mussolini by organizing a march from Munich to Berlin to overthrow the government collapsed under the fire of the Bavarian police.

Whether Kahr and Lossow had been willing to support Hitler is unclear. New evidence suggests that Tirpitz did not give up all hope of establishing a nationalist dictatorship for the time being. Contrary to other members of the former regime, he was always careful enough not be involved directly into the plots against the government, which were planned and submitted for his approval.

It was only in early 1924, after all his hopes of direct support by General Hans von Seeckt had been shattered that Tirpitz began to change his tactics. Instead of waiting behind the scenes for another plot to succeed, he now openly entered the political arena. Hesitantly, he accepted the offer of running as a candidate for the conservatives, the Deutsch-Nationale Volkspartei, in the general elections of May 1924. During his short campaign, he gave almost no speeches nor did he have anything like a political program. Instead he offered himself as "a simple soldier," who had nothing else in mind but the wish "to rally all national forces of our fatherland and to unite them regardless of any petty differences of opinion."[10] Similarly his views on foreign policy were vague, unrealistic, and dangerous. Like many rightists he was convinced that an alternative policy to the course of detente and international understanding advocated by Germany's Foreign Minister, Gustav Stresemann, was possible. Like them he did not shy away from a full-scale confrontation with France, for this seemed to be the only means to both save Germany's honor and fight out the terms for a peace treaty that would abolish the existing state of "slavery." However, in a climate that supported the German right, and drawing from his reputation as an unbending statesman, he won a respectable majority and entered the *Reichstag* as a conservative deputy in May 1924.

The conservative leadership hoped Tirpitz's reputation would enhance its chances of forming a coalition ranging from the extreme right to the Catholic Center Party. Greatly misjudging the attitude of the bourgeois parties, the conservative leadership suffered a severe defeat. Demanding the chancellorship for Tirpitz even before negotiations about forming a new government had begun was unacceptable for the middle parties. In spite of the other common grounds, they were afraid that Tirpitz's candidacy would provoke negative reactions abroad and undermine the constitutional powers of the president who was the only one to nominate a chancellor. Most importantly, Foreign Minister Stresemann from the Deutsche Volkspartei proved to be the strongest opponent of Tirpitz's chancellorship. In his eyes, any chance of improving Germany's position among the Great Powers would be gone if Tirpitz ever played a prominent role in German politics again. In order to strengthen his opposition towards Tirpitz, Stresemann probably asked Germany's envoys to foreign states to sound out how financial and political circles abroad would receive a prospective right-wing government or even Tirpitz's candidacy. The answers left no doubt about what would happen if the former Secretary of the Imperial Navy Office became chancellor. While the "Daily Telegraph" called Tirpitz's candidacy "a masterpiece of folly," the German ambassador in London, reported the "New York World," left no doubt about the reaction of the United States: "To any German who wishes his country to enjoy the benefit of an international loan, it must be sufficiently obvious that the mere mention of the bearded hero of the submarine offensive is madness pure and simple."[11]

Against this background, all attempts at forming a government under Tirpitz's leadership foundered. In spite of his belief that a change was necessary, Tirpitz stayed in the background and seems to have been reluctant to take office and full responsibility for domestic and foreign policy. Although he realized that the restrictions of his office in a multiparty coalition and the limitations of power under the given circumstances would have made it much more difficult to achieve his aims than most people expected, he nevertheless accused the leadership of the Deutsch-Nationale Volkspartei of mishandling his candidacy.

This notwithstanding, at the age of seventy-five Tirpitz was a remarkable figure in parliament. Many right-wing politicians and their voters still regarded him as the embodiment of German power politics, and though his real aims were unclear to most contemporaries as those of his naval policy had been to many before the war, he was a tough and cunning politician. Even his wavering attitude towards the Dawes Plan, to which he consented under pressure from leading industrialists and businessmen, did not harm his reputation. His opponents within in the Deutsch-Nationale Volkspartei only succeeded in thwarting the plan of electing Tirpitz chairman of the party. Instead, he became honorary chairman. Whether this was a far-reaching setback is doubtful. Tirpitz had not tried hard to become chairman. Moreover, this development only mirrored the deep split within the party. Tirpitz remained popular among the deputies as well as among the rank-and-file of the party.

This reputation remained his most important asset in his fight against what he regarded as a repetition of Germany's *Ohnmachtspolitik* (policy of powerlessness) before the war. His attempt to fight Stresemann, Germany's most successful foreign minister between 1923 and 1929, proved a failure. The Foreign Office attacked Tirpitz for publishing official documents without permission. An offical historian demanded Tirpitz be tried for treason because he had helped undermine Germany's fight against the war guilt charge. The storm caused by this scandal only died down after a few weeks.

It is difficult to say to what extent this scandal destroyed Tirpitz's chances to become chancellor or become Ebert's successor in the 1925 presidential elections. In spite of his disappointment, Tirpitz decided to support a strong nationalist in the presidential elections of spring 1925, which took place prematurely after President Ebert died unexpectedly. He helped to persuade Field Marshall Paul von Hindenburg, the hero of the Battle of Tannenberg, to run as conservative candidate in the second ballot. Though Hindenburg won the election by a small margin in May, Tirpitz's hopes were not fulfilled, at least not during his lifetime. Like many conservatives, he had hoped that it would be easy to manipulate Hindenburg who had been a successful military leader, but no politician. However, Hindenburg remained loyal to the constitution, refusing to reshape the Republic as a more authoritarian state. He even refused to dismiss the political advisers of his predecessor and replace them with loyal conservatives. Also, he ignored Tirpitz's demands to torpedo Stresemann's foreign policy.

Soon Tirpitz stepped into the background again, disappointed by party politics. In 1928, Tirpitz publicly announced that he would withdraw from the *Reichstag*. As in former times, he tried to exploit this very personal decision politically. In late May he published a private letter to a leading conservative, summarizing his political credo: "In our political life we have not made progress at all. I consider it wrong to blame this exclusively on our contemporary political system, as fatal as its effects are. The deepest cause of our political illness is, in my view, the lack of inner, psychological unity of our people. In spite of Bismarck, of our rise to world power, of the world war and breakdown, we have not built up of community of fate. [...] May everything that has been rebuilt artificially break down; Germany will live and resurge if it achieves inner national unity, the unity of a people sure of itself."[12]

In his eyes, the Republic of Weimar seemed unable to achieve this unity. In September 1929, only a few weeks before the Wall Street Crash shattered the political and economic foundations of the Republic, he wrote to a close friend: "Dictatorship and a tightening of the curb are necessary. [...] a chronic revolution is more deadly than an acute one."[13] This deep-seated conviction of the ills of democracy was the reason he occasionally participated in public rallies of the German right in spite of his age in 1929. In order to fight Stresemann's foreign policy, he joined the chairman of the Deutsch-Nationale Volkspartei, Alfred Hugenberg and Hitler in their anti-Young Plan campaign.

While the impact of his second career as a "grey excellence" on German politics is difficult to measure, there can be no doubt that his reputation was still great enough to deeply influence the new navy, the *Reichsmarine*.

The activities of the naval archives were responsible for this impact; they began publishing a history of the "War at Sea" in 1920. Written exclusively by naval officers and not, as Captain Otto Groos sarcastically remarked in his memoirs, by "arm-chair strategists like Professor Delbrück,"[14] These volumes proved extremely influential.

The *Seekriegswerk* was an open approval of Tirpitz's ideas. The *Marineleitung* and the director of the naval archives, Rear Admiral Mantey, discussed all aspects of the war at sea with Tirpitz before the respective volumes were published.

In 1931, Mantey admitted that it was difficult to overcome the "master" and his ideas. To the former chief of the Naval Cabinet, Admiral Müller, he wrote: "Writing naval history is much more complicated than outsiders can imagine, if one wants to tell the truth on the one hand and not to hurt the old navy on the other."[15] Though high-ranking fellow officers and younger officers had occasionally criticized his naval policy and the foundations of his strategic concept, Tirpitz could be satisfied. The leadership of the *Reichsmarine* admired him and remained loyal to his basic ideas. Admiral Erich Raeder, one of Tirpitz's greatest admirers who had taken over command of the *Reichsmarine* in 1928, suppressed critical studies dealing with naval policy and naval strategy as well as the deficiencies of naval command before and during the Great War. When Tirpitz celebrated his eightieth birthday in 1929, former Vice Admiral Adolf von Trotha praised Tirpitz's achievements and his legacy to future generations: "A people of 70 million in the heart of Europe, born by both German strength of mind and faith, cannot be suppressed by any power in the world. Today we solemnly swear and are grateful to your Excellency from the bottom of our hearts to work for this German aim."[16]

In the late 1920s Tirpitz could also be satisfied with his private life. Whereas he had been a rather poor man in the early 1920s, his financial situation had slowly improved in the meantime. In 1928, he left Saint Blasien in the Black Forest, which had been his beloved summer resort for more than two decades and moved to Feldafing at Lake Starnberg. There he spent the remaining years of his life. On March 6, 1930, he died in his new home after a heart attack.

His state funeral in Munich emphasized the importance of his personal achievements and the validity of his ideas. Apart from representatives of the army and the navy, many right-wing groups, including Hitler's SS, assembled on the cemetery using this occasion as a demonstration against the Republic and for far-reaching political aims. Former Vice Admiral Trotha again praised Tirpitz. "It is our duty to victoriously carry the legacy of the Grand Admiral into the German future."[17]

Aftermath

At the turn of the last century, Grand Admiral Alfred von Tirpitz was at the center of major world events. He had planned the build-up of a powerful navy that was capable of successfully challenging Britain's supremacy and fulfilling the dreams of many of his contemporaries who hoped that the twentieth century would be a century of German dominance. "A supreme tactician he even adhered to a losing strategy like a chess player increasing his material advantage while overlooking a mortal attack on his king,"[1] Raphael Scheck said. Tirpitz always claimed that he had not failed but that "the German people did not understand the sea."[2] He was wrong just as much as his assumptions had been, but he would never admit failure. Instead, when his strategy proved wrong and he was dismissed, Tirpitz became a politician. During World War I and the 1920s he hoped to achieve his life's aim by paving the way for an authoritarian regime. After his death, the man he had convinced to run for president in 1925, Field-Marshall Paul von Hindenburg, opened the floodgates for the enemies of the Weimar Republic by installing a presidential cabinet, which proved the first step on the road to total disaster.

Against this background, Tirpitz's shadow still loomed large among members of the German right and the navy. Although he had completely failed as a naval officer and politician during his lifetime, it was others who were held responsible. For many, he was still the man who had tried to unite Germany and become a leading power in the world. Thus a statue was erected in Berlin as a reminder of Tirpitz's aims to future generations: "Germany must become powerful and free again."[3] The presence of President Hindenburg emphasized that many members of the nation's leadership still shared this conviction.[4]

Raeder and the *Kriegsmarine* entered into Tirpitz's heritage. Though Raeder had doubts about the wisdom of Tirpitz's battle fleet concept in the mid-1930s, he never seriously questioned the latter's main idea—the conviction that naval power was the most important requirement for a nation that aspired to becoming a leading power in the world. This conviction was the basis of an alliance with Hitler, who had come to power in 1933. On April 1, 1939, Hitler baptized a battleship, (Tirpitz,) openly challenging Great Britain once again. The disaster that followed was by far greater than the one Germany had experienced in the Tirpitz-era. In 1945, the country lay in ruins and Tirpitz's statue had been melted into ammunitions. Moreover, it was more than a strange irony of fate that the street that had been named after Tirpitz in the center of Berlin, changed its name to "Reichpietsch Embankment," in memory of Max Reichpietsch—a sailor who had been excuted for leading a mutiny against the naval leadership in 1917. By remembering Max Reichpietsch, the Social Democratic Party wanted to lay the foundations of a new democratic and peaceful tradition in Germany.

German naval historiography had difficulty dismissing old views and convictions despite the dramatic and fundamental changes of 1945. Until the mid-1960s, Tirpitz was by and large still regarded as an admiral whose aims had been fully legitimate and could not be blamed for the shortcomings of politicians. It took another generation to judge Tirpitz accurately: one of the architects of a policy that led to the catastrophes of the twentieth century. When the building of the former Imperial Navy Office was turned into the official residence of the German Ministry of Defence in Berlin after unification, the government took great care to avoid irritating the public by revoking old traditions.

Accordingly, the German Minister of Defence neither resides in Tirpitz's nor Scheer's office, and though the main entrance is from the Stauffenbergstraße, named after the leader of the military plot against Hitler, the Reichpietsch Embankment still runs behind the Ministry of Defence. It is only a question of time until the Tirpitz Pier at Kiel's naval port will be renamed.

Notes

Chapter 1: Young Tirpitz

1. Albert Scheibe, *Tirpitz* (Lübeck: Charles Coleman, 1934), 4–5;
    Helene d'Alton-Rauch, *Von den Ahnen Alfred v. Tirpitz* [From the
    Alfred von Tirpitz Ancestors] (Berlin: Druck und Berlag von U.
    Weichert, 1935), 331–332; Ulrich von Hassel, *Tirpitz: Sein Leben
    und Wirken mit Berücksichtigung sei-ner Beziehungen zu Albrecht
    von Stosch* [Tirpitz: His Life and Work especially with regard to his
    Relationship with Albrecht von Stosch.] (Stuttgart: Belsersche Verlag
    1920), 66–68.

2. Rolf Hobson and Eva Besteck, "Tirpitz Papers N 253," (BA-MA,
    2004), 114

3. Albert Scheibe, *Tirpitz* (Lübeck: Charles Coleman, 1934), 7; Hassell,
    *Tirpitz: Sein Leben und Wirken mit Berücksichtigung sei-ner
    Beziehungen zu Albrecht von Stosch* [Tirpitz: His Life and Work
    especially with regard to his Relationship with Albrecht von Stosch.]
    (Stuttgart: Belsersche Verlag 1920), 70–73.

4. Alfred von Tirpitz, *My Memoirs* [Meine Denkschriften] 2 vols. (Lon-
    don: Hurst & Blackett, 1919), 1–2.

5. Ibid.

Chapter 2: An Able and Ambitious Naval Officer

1. *Terrell D. Gottschall, By Order of the Kaiser: Otto von Diederichs and
    the Rise of the Imperial German Navy, 1865–1902* (Washington,
    D.C.: U.S. Naval Institute Press, 2003), 12.

2. Tirpitz, *My Memoirs* 1, (London: Hurst & Blackett, 1919), 4–5.

3. Ibid., 2–3.

4. Ibid., 3.

5. Ibid., 4.

6. Cited in Gottschall, *By Order of the Kaiser*, 15.

7. For details cf. Gottschall, *By Order of the Kaiser*.

8. Cf. the manuscripts in the collection of Tirpitz Papers in the *Deutsche Schiffahrtsmuseum* at Bremerhaven.

9. For copies of these letters cf. Tirpitz Papers N 253, 384–386.

10. Tirpitz to his parents June 27, 1865, in: Tirpitz Papers N 253, 384.

11. Cf. Gottschall, *By Order of the Kaiser*, 17–25. This account is based on Diederichs' logbook.

12. Hassell, *Tirpitz*, 77.

13. Tirpitz, *My Memoirs* 1, 4.

14. Gottschall, *By Order of the Kaiser*, 25.

15. Tirpitz, *My Memoirs* 1, 5.

16. Tirpitz, *My Memoirs* 1, 4–34.; Hassell, *Tirpitz*, 76–91.

17. Cf. Lambi, *The Navy and German Power Politics, 1862–1914*, 2–3.

18. Tirpitz, *My Memoirs* 1, 18.

19. Tirpitz to his parents, November 2, 1868 and February 7, 1868, in: Tirpitz Papers N 253, 384.

20. Cf. Gottschall, *By Order of the Kaiser*, 28.

21. Tirpitz, *My Memoirs* 1, 6.

22. Tirpitz to his parents, July 18, 1870, in: Tirpitz Papers N 253, 385.

23. Tirpitz, *My Memoirs* 1, 6–8

24. Ibid., 7.

25. Ibid., 8.

26. Ibid. 9. Cf. also Tirpitz's letters to his parents, in which he scornfully describes this drill. In: Tirpitz Papers, N 253, 385.

27. Tirpitz to his parents, July 16, 1870, in: Tirpitz Papers N 253, 385.

28. Tirpitz to his parents, January 23,1871, in: Tirpitz Papers N 253, 385.

29. Cf. the letters he wrote to his parents in fall 1870, early 1871, ibid.

30. Tirpitz to his father, September 11, 1871, ibid. Also cited in: Hassell, *Tirpitz*, 88–91.

31. Tirpitz, *My Memoirs*, 1–14.

32. Cf. His letters in: Tirpitz Papers N 253, 385–386.

33. Tirpitz to his parents, January 27, 1873, in: Tirpitz Papers N 253, 387.

34. Cf. Gottschall, *By Order of the Kaiser*, 43–44.
35. Cited in: Schulze-Hinrichs, *Tirpitz*, 12.

Chapter 3: A Man of New Ideas
 1. Tirpitz, *My Memoirs* 1, 26.
 2. Ibid., 35.
 3. Cited in: Kelly, *Tirpitz*, 221.
 4. Scheck, *Tirpitz*, 2.
 5. Tirpitz, *My Memoirs* 1, 35.
 6. Ibid., 49.
 7. Tirpitz to Caprivi, March 13, 1888, cited in: Kelly, *Tirpitz*, 237.
 8. Tirpitz, *My Memoirs* 1, 27–31
 9. Ibid., 30.
10. Berghahn, *Tirpitz-Plan*, 58. Cited and translated by Kelly, *Tipitz*, 240.
11. Cf. the letters to his daughter Ilse
12. Wilhelm II to the French ambassador, the Marquis de Noailles, on October 28, 1899. Cited in: Lambi, *The Navy and German Power Politics, 1862–1914*, 155.
13. Cited in Lambi, *The Navy and German Power Politics, 1862–1914*, 34.
14. Tirpitz to Stosch, October 12, 1877. Cited in: Kelly, *Tirpitz*, 221.
15. Tirpitz, *My Memoirs* 1, 47.
16. Ibid., 53.
17. *Dienstschrift* no IX, cited in: Hobson, *Imperialism: A Study*, 206.
18. Ibid., 208.
19. Cf. ibid, 31–124; Lambi, *The Navy and German Power Politics, 1862–1914*, 84–86, 114–116.

Chapter 4: In the Center of Power
 1. Tirpitz, *My Memoirs* 1, 91.
 2. Cited in: Lambi, *The Navy and German Power Politics, 1862–1914*, 140.
 3. Ibid.
 4. Tirpitz, *My Memoirs* 1, 93.
 5. Ibid., 110–111.

6. Tirpitz, *My Memoirs* 1, 97.

7. Tirpitz to Senden, February 15, 1896. Cited in: Steinberg, *Yesterday's Deterrent: Tirpitz and the Birth of the German Battle Fleet*, 130.

8. Ibid., 113.

9. Ibid., 110.

10. Grand Duke Friedrich von Baden to Chancellor Hohenlohe, August 23, 1897. Cited in: Steinberg, *Yesterday's Deterrent: Tirpitz and the Birth of the German Battle Fleet*, 141.

11. Bülow to Prince Eulenburg, December 26, 1897. Cited in: Lambi, *The Navy and German Power Politics, 1862–1914*, 157.

12. Bülow to Friedrich A. Krupp, May 22, 1898. Cited in: Lambi, *The Navy and German Power Politics, 1862–1914.*

13. Reprinted in: Steinberg, *Yesterday's Deterrent: Tirpitz and the Birth of the German Battle Fleet*, 209—221, though wrongly dated.

14. Berghahn, *Germany and the Approach of War in 1914*, 34; Lambi, *The Navy and German Power Politics, 1862–1914*, 140.

15. Tirpitz to Eisendecher, August 31, 1897. Cited in: Lambi, *The Navy and German Power Politics, 1862–1914*, 141–142.

16. Tirpitz, *My Memoirs* 1, 115.

17. Ibid., 116.

18. Steinberg, *Yesterday's Deterrent: Tirpitz and the Birth of the German Battle Fleet*, 147.

19. Cited ibid.

20. Steinberg, *Yesterday's Deterrent: Tirpitz and the Birth of the German Battle Fleet*, 160–161.

21. Scheck, *Tirpitz*, xii.

22. Steinberg, *Yesterday's Deterrent: Tirpitz and the Birth of the German Battle Fleet*, 164.

23. Ibid., 165.

24. Cited ibid., 59–60.

25. Cited ibid., 173.

26. Tirpitz, *My Memoirs* 1, 116.

27. Tirpitz to the Kaiser, September 28, 1899, cited in: Lambi, *The Navy and German Power Politics, 1862–1914*, 139.

28. Ibid., 146.

29. Preamble of the second navy bill, June 14, 1900. Cited in: Lambi, *The Navy and German Power Politics, 1862–1914*, 147.

30. Tirpitz, *My Memoirs* 1, 126.

31. Cf. the speech of Wilhelm II at the launching of the ship-of-the-line *Wittelsbach* in Wilhelmshaven, July 3, 1900. Cited in: Johann Ernst, *Reden des Kaisers* [Speeches by the Emperor] (Verl: German Paperbacks, 1966), 81.

32. Bülow to F.A. Krupp, May 22, 1898, in: Krupp-Archives, FAH III B 145.

33. Cf. Tirpitz, *My Memoirs* 1, 195.

34. Szögyeny to Goluchowski, February 5, 1900. Cited in: Kennedy, *Rise of Anglo-German Antagonism*, 241.

35. Hobson, *Imperialism at Sea: Naval Strategic Thought, the Ideology of Sea Power and the Tirpitz Plan, 1875–1914*, 266.

36. Berghahn, *Germany and the Approach of War in 1914*, 38–39.

37. Scheck, *Tirpitz*, xii.

38. Tirpitz to Richthofen, November 1, 1904. Cited in: Tirpitz, *My Memoirs* 1, 169.

39. Cf. Herwig, *The German Reaction*, 278.

40. Lambi, *The Navy and German Power Politics, 1862–1914*, 280–281.

41. Ibid.

42. Trotha to Tirpitz, March 18, 1908, cited in: Lambi, *The Navy and German Power Politics, 1862–1914*, 295.

43. Tirpitz, *Politische Dokumente* 1, 84.

44. Wilhelm II to Lord Tweedmouth, February 16, 1908, quoted in: Bartholdy, Albrecht, and Johannes Lepsius, and Friedrich Thimme, eds. *Die Große Politik der Europäischen Kabinette von 1871–1914.* [The Foreign Policy of European Cabinets, 1871–1914], 24, 32–35.

45. Wilhelm II to Bülow, August 13, 1908, ibid., 126–129.

46. Bülow to Holstein, August 16, 1908, cited in: Lambi, *The Navy and German Power Politics, 1862–1914*, 295.

47. Bülow to Tirpitz, November 30, 1908. Cited in: Lambi, *The Navy and German Power Politics, 1862–1914,* 296.

48. Undated note, in: BA-MA Tirpitz Papers N 253, 9.

49. Tirpitz to Bülow, December 17, 1908. Cited in: Lambi, *The Navy and German Power Politics, 1862–1914,* 296.

50. Tirpitz to Bülow, January 4, 1909. Cited in: Lambi, *The Navy and German Power Politics, 1862–1914*, 297

51. Ibid.

52. Marginal comment on Tirpitz's letter of January 20, 1909. cited in: Bartholdy, Albrecht, and Johannes Lepsius, and Friedrich Thimme, eds. *Die Große Politik der Europäischen Kabinette von 1871–1914* 28. [The Foreign Policy of European Cabinets, 1871–1914 28], 70.

53. Note by Tirpitz April 3, 1909, cited in: Lambi, *The Navy and German Power Politics, 1862–1914*, 299–300.

54. Protocol of a conference held on June 3, 1909 in the Chancellor's office, cited in: Bartholdy, Albrecht, and Johannes Lepsius, and Friedrich Thimme, eds. *Die Große Politik der Europäischen Kabinette von 1871–1914* 28. [The Foreign Policy of European Cabinets, 1871–1914 28], 50.

55. Tirpitz to Capelle, September 19, 1909, in: BA-MA Tirpitz Papers N 253, 8.

56. Tirpitz, *My Memoirs* 1, 137.

57. Tirpitz, *My Memoirs* 1, 211.

58. Tirpitz to the Chancellor, August 30, 1911, cited in: Tirpitz, *Politische Dokumente* 1, 208.

59. Tirpitz, *My Memoirs* 1, 213.

60. Cf. Tirpitz's notes for his *Immediatvortrag* in: BA-MA Tirpitz Papers N 253, 25; Berghahn, *Germany and the Approach of War in 1914*, 106.

61. Wilhelm II to Bethmann Hollweg, September 26, 1911. Cited in: Tirpitz, *Politische Dokumente* 1, 216.

62. Tirpitz to Bethmann Hollweg, October 7, 1911. Cited in: Lambi, *The Navy and German Power Politics, 1862–1914*, 366.

63. Tirpitz to Bethmann Hollweg, October 7, 1911. Cited in: Berghahn, *Germany and the Approach of War in 1914*, 107–108.

64. Heeringen (Chief of the Admiralty Staff) to Bethmann Hollweg, October 7, 1911. Cited in: Berghahn, *Germany and the Approach of War in 1914*, 108.

65. Speech by Heydebrand in the *Reichstag*, November 9, 1911. Cited in: Berghahn, *Germany and the Approach of War in 1914*, 114.

66. Berghahn, *Germany*, 119.

67. Tirpitz, *My Memoirs* 1, 215.

68. Bethmann Hollweg to the Badenese minister in Berlin, March 12, 1912. Cited in: Lambi, *The Navy and German Power Politics, 1862–1914*, 371.

69. Cf. Haldane's diary of his visit to Berlin, February 9, 1912, cited in: British Documents 6, 680.

70. Tirpitz, *My Memoirs* 1, 222.

71. Diary of Captain Hopman, February 10, 1912, cited in: Hopman, *Albert Hopman: Das ereignisreiche Leben eines "Wilhelminers."* *Tagebücher, Briefe, Aufzeichnungen 1901–1920* [Albert Hopman: The Life of a 'Wilhelminer.' Diaries, Letters, and Notes 1901–1920], 198.

72. Ibid., 197, diary entry of February 9, 1912.

73. Kennedy, Anglo-German Antagonism, 451.

74. Memo by Sir Edward Grey, February 22, 1912. Cited in: *British Documents* 6, 696.

75. Epkenhans, *Die wilhelminische Flottenrüstung 1908–1914. Welt-machtstre-ben, industrieller Fortschritt, soziale Integration* [Naval Policy in the Wilhelmine Era, 1908–1914: The Grasp for World Power, Industrial Progress, and Social Integration], 325–336.

76. Tirpitz to Capelle, July 8, 1913, cited in: Berghahn, *Germany and the Approach of War in 1914*, 128.

77. Speech by Tirpitz, October 9, 1913, in: Tirpitz Papers N 253, 423.

78. Winston S. Churchill, *World Crisis 1*, 143–44.

79. Epkenhans, *Die wilhelminische Flottenrüstung 1908–1914. Welt-machtstre-ben, industrieller Fortschritt, soziale Integration* [Naval Policy in the Wilhelmine Era, 1908–1914: The Grasp for World Power, Industrial Progress, and Social Integration], 328–330.

80. Cf. the report by Captain v. Müller, October 30, 1913, in: BA-MA RM 3/3707, and the Kaiser's letter to Tirpitz, November 4, 1913, BA-MA, RM 2/1765.

81. Cf. Tirpitz's note about his conversation with the Kaiser, March 11, 1912. Cited in: Tirpitz, *Politische Dokumente* 1, 324.

82. Undated note, May 1914, in: BA-MA Tirpitz Papers N 253/29.

83. Comment on a memo prepared by Vice-Admiral Capelle, May 17, 1914, ibid.

84. Cf. the diary of Admiral v. Müller, May 19, 1914, in: BA-MA N 159/4.

85. Notes for an *Immediatvortrag*, May 17, 1914 (not held, postponed to a later date), BA-MA Tirpitz Papers N 253/29.

86. Diary of Captain Hopman, June 15, 1914, cited in: Hopman, *Albert Hopman: Das ereignisreiche Leben eines "Wilhelminers." Tagebücher, Briefe, Aufzeichnungen 1901–1920* [Albert Hopman: The Life of a 'Wilhelminer.' Diaries, Letters, and Notes 1901–1920], 377.

87. Hopman diary, July 29–30, 1914, cited in: ibid., 404–405.

88. Tirpitz, *My Memoirs* 1, 283–284.

89. Operations order no. 1, July 30, 1914. Cited in: Lambi, *The Navy and German Power Politics, 1862–1914*, 422.

90. Tirpitz, *My Memoirs* 1, 287.

91. Ibid., 268–269.

92. Kennedy, *Anglo-German Antagonism*, 423.

Chapter 5: Failure

1. Tirpitz to his wife, September 24, 1914, 466.

2. Tirpitz to his wife, August 21, 1914. Cited in: Tirpitz, *My Memoirs* 2, 453.

3. Tirpitz to his wife, October 8, 1914. Cited in: Tirpitz, *My Memoirs* 2, 474–475.

4. Tirpitz to his wife, August 20, 1914. Cited in: Tirpitz, *My Memoirs* 2, 453.

5. Ibid., 366.

6. Pohl to Ingenohl, August 30, 1914. Cited in: Tirpitz, *Politische Dokumente* 2, 77.

7. Cf. Tirpitz's "Memo on naval warfare in the North Sea," August 15, 1914. Cited in: Tirpitz, *Politische Dokumente* 2, 53–55.

8. Cf. Hopman diary, entry of November 10, 1914, 492–493.

9. Cf. Hopman Diary, entry of July 30, 1914, p. 406; cf. also Tirpitz's letter to the Kaiser, August 6, 1914, citied in: Tirpitz, *Politische Dokumente* 2, 42.

10. Citied in: Georg Alexander von Müller, *Regierte der Kaiser?* (Berlin: Musterschmidt-Verlag, 1959), 49.

11. Tirpitz to his wife, August 30, 1914, cited in: Tirpitz, *My Memoirs* 2, 457.

12. Ibid., 474.

13. Tirpitz to his wife, September 28,1914, cited in: Tirpitz, *My Memoirs* 2, 469.

14. Citied in: Herwig, *"Luxury" Fleet: The Imperial German Navy 1888–1918*, 151.

15. Diary entry by Captain Hopman, January 8, 1915. Cited in: Hopman, *Albert Hopman: Das ereignisreiche Leben eines "Wilhelminers." Tagebücher, Briefe, Aufzeichnungen 1901–1920* [Albert Hopman: The Life of a 'Wilhelminer.' Diaries, Letters, and Notes 1901–1920], 541—542.

16. Ibid., 396.

17. Tirpitz to Müller, January 25, 1915, cited in: Tirpitz, *Politische Dokumente* 2, 198–200.

18. Letter by Tirpitz and Bachmann to Müller, February 16, 1915. Cited in: Gerhard, *Die deutsche Seekriegsleitung im Ersten Weltkrieg* [The German Naval High Command during World War I] no. 317.

19. Tirpitz to Bethmann Hollweg, January 19, 1915, in: BA-MA RM 3/11495.

20. Tirpitz to his wife, July 2, 1915. Cited in: Tirpitz, *My Memoirs* 2, 536.

21. Tirpitz, *My Memoirs* 2, 330.

22. Tirpitz, *My Memoirs* 2, 399.

23. Ibid., 415.

24. Ibid, 407, 412–413.

25. Cited in: Tirpitz, *My Memoirs* 2, 416.

26. Tirpitz to Falkenhayn, February 13, 1916, cited in: Tirpitz, *My Memoirs* 2, 419.

27. Ibid., 420.

28. Scheck, *Tirpitz*, 42–43.

29. Scheck, *Tirpitz*, 48–81.

30. Trotha to Eulenburg, October 20, 1916. Cited in: Scheck, *Tirpitz*, 55.

31. Ludendorff to Tirpitz's son Wolfgang in 1921, Scheck, *Tirpitz*, 59.

32. Ibid., 67.

33. Ibid.

34. Tirpitz to Prince Max, October 17, 1918. Cited in: Tirpitz, *My Memoirs* 2, 337.

Chapter 6: Grey Excellence
1. Tirpitz, *My Memoirs* 2, 445.
2. Ibid., 449.
3. Ibid., 514.
4. Tirpitz, *My Memoirs* 2, 448–449.
5. Ibid., 450.
6. Prince Henry to Tirpitz, October 29, 1919 and Tirpitz's answer, November 1919, both in: BA-MA Tirpitz Papers N 253, 183.
7. For details cf. Scheck, *Tirpitz*, 82–212.
8. Cited in: Scheck, *Tirpitz*, 98.
9. Cited in: Scheck, *Tirpitz*, 103.
10. Speech by Tirpitz in Königsberg, December 7, 1924, clipping of the Ostpreußische Zeitung, in: BA-MA Tirpitz Papers N 253, 216.
11. Cited in: Scheck, *Tirpitz*, 156.
12. Tirpitz to Westarp, March 10, 1928, cited in: Scheck, *Tirpitz*, 206–207.
13. Tirpitz to Scheibe, September 16, 1929, cited in: Scheibe, *Tirpitz*, 61.
14. Groos, Memoirs (unpublished), BA-MA Groos papers N 165, 20.
15. Mantey to Müller, October 19, 1932. Cited in: Rahn, *Strategische Optionen* [Strategic Options], 207.
16. Cited in: Trotha, *Tirpitz*, 169.
17. Ibid., 171.

Chapter 7: Aftermath
1. Scheck, *Tirpitz*, 6.
2. Tirpitz, *My Memoirs* 2, 445.
3. Speech by former Captain Widenmann, 31.5.1931, Widenmann papers, BA-MA N 158/4.
4. Cf. Bird, *Erich Raeder: Admiral of the Third Reich*.

Selected Bibliography

Books on Tirpitz and the Imperial German Navy are innumerable. The following selection should suffice to provide the general reader with further information on his times and his policy.

Assmann, Kurt. *Deutsche Seestrategie in zwei Weltkriegen* [*German Naval Strategy in Two World Wars*] Heidelberg: Kurt Vohwinckel Verlag, 1957.

Bartholdy, Albrecht, and Johannes Lepsius, and Friedrich Thimme, eds. *Die Große Politik der Europäischen Kabinette von 1871–1914* [The Foreign Policy of European Cabinets, 1871–1914] (Berlin: Deutsche Verlagsgesellschaft, 1922–1927).

Berghahn, Volker R. *Der Tirpitz-Plan: Genesis und Verfall einer innenpoliti-schen Krisenstrategie unter Wilhelm II* [The Tirpitz Plan: Rise and Fall of a domestic-political crisis-strategy under Wilhelm II]. Translated by (Düsseldorf: Droste-Verlag, 1971).

———. *Germany and the Approach of War in 1914* (New York: St. Martin's Press, 1973).

———. *Imperial Germany 1871–1914: Economy, Society, Culture, and Politics* (Providence-Oxford: Berghahn Books, 1994).

Bird, Keith. *Erich Raeder: Admiral of the Third Reich* (Annapolis: Naval Institute Press, 2006).

Birnbaum, Karl. *Peace Moves and U-Boat Warfare: A Study of Imperial Ger-many's Policy towards the United States April 18, 1916–January 9, 1917* (Stockholm: Almquist & Wiksell, 1958).

Bueb, Volkmar. *Die "junge Schule" der französischen Marine: Strategie und Politik 1875-1900* [The Young School of French Naval Strategy: Strategy and Politics, 1875-1900] (Boppard: Boldt-Verlag, 1971).

Canis, Konrad. *Von Bismarck zur Weltpolitik: Deutsche Außenpolitik 1890–1902.* [From Bismarck to World Politics: German Foreign Policy, 1890–1902] (Berlin: Akademie-Verlag, 1997).

Churchill, Winston S. *World Crisis* 1 (London: Odhams Press, 1938).

Deist, Wilhelm. *Flottenpolitik und Flottenpropaganda: Das Nachrichtenbureau des Reichsmarineamtes 1897–1914.* [Naval Policy and Naval Propaganda: The News Bureau of the Imperial Navy Office, 1897–1914] (Stuttgart: Deutsche Verlagsanstalt, 1976).

Deist, William and Annika Mombauer, eds. *The Kaiser and 'his' Navy, 1888–1918,* in: *The Kaiser: New Research on Wilhelm's Role in Imperial Germany* (Cam-bridge: University Press, 2003), 12–36.

Duppler, Jörg. *Der Juniorpartner: England und die Entwicklung der Deutschen Marine 1848–1890* [The Junior Partner: England and the Development of the German Navy, 1848–1890] (Herford: Mittler & Sohn, 1985).

Epkenhans, Michael. *Alfred von Tirpitz (1849–1930),* in *Das Kaiserreich. Portrait einer Epoche in Biographien.* ed. by Michael Fröhlich (Darmstadt, Germany: Wissenschaftliche Buchgesellschaft 2001), 228–239.

——. *Die Kaiserliche Marine im Ersten Weltkrieg: Weltmacht oder Unter-gang?* [The German Navy during World War I: World Power Status or Fall?] in: *Der Erste Welt-krieg: Wirkung, Wahrnehmung* [The First War: Effect, Perception, Analysis] Ed. by Wolfgang Michalka, (München: Piper, 1994), 319–340

——. *Die wilhelminische Flottenrüstung 1908–1914. Welt-machtstre-ben, industrieller Fortschritt, soziale Integration* [Naval Policy in the Wilhelmine Era, 1908–1914: The Grasp for World Power, Industrial Progress, and Social Integration] (München: Oldenbourg-Verlag, 1991).

Gooch, G.P. and Harold Temperley, eds. *British Documents on the Origins of the War 1898–1914* 6 (London: H. M. Stationery Office, 1930).

Granier, Gerhard, ed. *Die deutsche Seekriegsleitung im Ersten Weltkrieg* [The German Naval High Command during World War I], 4 vols. (Koblenz: Bundesarchiv, 1999–2004).

Halpern, Paul G. *A Naval History of World War I* (London: Routledge, 1995).

Hassel, Ulrich von. *Tirpitz: Sein Leben und Wirken mit Berücksichtigung sei-ner Beziehungen zu Albrecht von Stosch* [Tirpitz: His Life and Work especially with regard to his Relationship with Albrecht von Stosch] (Stuttgart: Deutsche Verlagsanstalt, 1920).

Herwig, Holger H. *"Luxury" Fleet: The Imperial German Navy 1888–1918*, (London: Ashfield, 1980).

———. *The Failure of German Sea Power 1914–1945: Mahan, Tirpitz, and Raeder Reconsidered*, in The International History Review X, no. 1, (1988): 691–705

———. *The German Reaction to the Dreadnought Revolution*, in *The International History Review* XIII, no. 2, (1991): 273–283.

Hobson, Rolf. *Imperialism at Sea: Naval Strategic Thought, the Ideology of Sea Power and the Tirpitz Plan, 1875–1914* (Boston-Leiden: Brill, 2002).

Hopman, Albert. *Albert Hopman: Das ereignisreiche Leben eines "Wilhelminers." Tagebücher, Briefe, Aufzeichnungen 1901–1920* [Albert Hopman: The Life of a 'Wilhelminer.' Diaries, Letters, and Notes 1901–1920.] Ed. by Michael Epkenhans. (Munich: Oldenbourg Verlag, 2004).

Hubatsch, Walther. *Die Ära Tirpitz: Studien zur deutschen Marinepolitik 1890–1918* [The Tirpitz Era: Studies on German Naval Policy, 1890-1914] (Göttingen: Musterschmidt, 1955).

Kaulisch, Baldur. *Alfred von Tirpitz und die imperialistische deutsche Flotten-rü-stung: Eine politische Biographie. [Alfred von Tirpitz and the imperialist German Naval Build-up.]*, 2nd. ed. (Berlin: Militärverlag, 1982).

Kelly, Patrick J. *Tirpitz and the Development of the German Torpedo Arm, 1877–1889*, in *New Interpretations in Naval History*, ed. by Robert W. Love Jr., Laurie Bogle, Brian VaDeMark, and Maochun Yu. (Annapolis: Naval Institute Press, 2001), 219–249.

Kennedy, Paul M. *Rise of the Anglo-German Antagonism, 1860–1914* (London: George Allen & Unwin, 1980).

———. *Tirpitz, England, and the Second Navy Law of 1900: A Strategical Critique*, in *Militärgeschichtliche Mitteilungen* 8 [Proceedings on Military History], (1970): 33–57.

———. *Maritime Strategieprobleme der deutsch-englischen Flottenrivalität. [Strategic Problems of the Anglo-German Naval Rivalry]*, in *Marine und Marinepolitik 1871–1914*, ed. by Herbert Schottelius and Wilhelm Deist, (Düsseldorf: Droste, 1981): 178–210.

Lambi, Ivo N. *The Navy and German Power Politics 1862–1914* (London: George Allen & Unwin, 1984).

Marder, Arthur J. *The Anatomy of British Sea Power: A History of British Naval Policy in the Pre-Dreadnought Era, 1880–1905* (Hamden, CT: Archon Books, 1964).

Osborne, Eric W. *The Battle of Heligoland Bight* (Bloomington: Indiana University Press, 2006).

Rahn, Werner. Strategische Optionen und Erfahrungen der deutschen Marineführung 1914 bis 1944: Zu den Chancen und Grenzen einer mitteleuropäischen Kontinentalmacht gegen Seemächte [Strategical Options and Experiences of Germany's Naval Leadership, 1914-1944: Opportunities and Limitations of a Continental Power towards Sea Powers], in Werner Rahn ed., Deutsche Marinen im Wandel. Vom Symbol nationaler Einheit zum Instrument internationaler Sicherheit [German Navies in a Changing World. From a Symbol of National Unity to an Instrument of International Security], (Munich: Oldenbourg, 2005), 197–233.

Reichsarchiv, ed. *Der Weltkrieg: Kriegsrüstung und Kriegswirtschaft* 1 [The World War: Armaments and War Economy 1] (Berlin: Reichsdruckerei, 1930).

Röhl, John C.G. *Wilhelm II: Der Aufbau der persönlichen Monarchie 1888–1900* [Wilhelm II: The Structure of the Personal Monarchy] (München: Beck-Verlag, 2001).

Berghahn, Volker R. and Wilhelm Deist, ed. *Rüstung im Zeichen der wilhelminischen Weltpolitik: Grundlegende Dokumente 1890–1914* [Armaments in the Era of German World Policy: Basic Documents, 1890–1914] (Düsseldorf: Droste, 1988).

Salewski, Michael: *Tirpitz: Aufstieg, Macht, Scheitern* [Tirpitz: Rise, Power, and Failure] (Göttingen: Musterschmidt, 1979).

Scheck, Raphael. *Alfred von Tirpitz and German Right-Wing Politics, 1914–1930.* N J: University of North Carolina Press, 1998).

Scheibe, Albert. *Tirpitz* (Lübeck: Charles Coleman, 1934).

Steinberg, Jonathan. *Yesterday's Deterrent: Tirpitz and the Birth of the German Bat-tle Fleet* (London: MacDonald, 1968).

Tirpitz, Alfred von. *My Memoirs.* 2 Vols., (London: Hurst & Blackett, 1919).

——. *Politische Dokumente* 1: *Der Aufbau der deutschen Weltmacht* [*Political Documents: The Build-up of German World Power*] (Stuttgart-Berlin: Cotta, 1924).

——*Politische Dokumente* 2: *Deutsche Ohnmachtspolitik im Weltkriege* [Political Documents 2: German Policy Impotence in World Wars] (Hamburg-Berlin: Hanseatische Verlagsanstalt, 1926).

Trotha, Adolf von, Großadmiral von Tirpitz [Grand Admiral von Tirpitz] (Breslau: Korn Verlag,1933).

Uhle-Wettler, Franz. *Alfred von Tirpitz in seiner Zeit* [Alfred von Tirpitz in his times] (Hamburg: Mittler & Sohn, 1998).

Winzen, Peter. *Bülows Weltmachtkonzept: Untersuchungen zur Frühphase seiner Außenpolitik 1897–1901* [Bülow's Concept of World Policy: A Study on the early Phase of his Foreign Policy, 1897–1901] (Boppard: Boldt, 1977).

About the Author

Dr. Michael Epkenhans is the Director of the Otto Von Bismarck Foundation in Friedrichsruh near Hamburg and Associate Professor at Hamburg University. His Ph.D. thesis on "Wilhelminische Flottenrüstung 1908–1914" was awarded the University Prize of Münster University in 1991. His habilitation "Albert Hopman: Das ereignisreiche Leben eines 'Wilhelminers'" (2004), deals with the life of a German Admiral in the Tirpitz Era. He also published the private letters of Admiral Reinhard Scheer (2006), as well as a number of articles on German military and naval history in the nineteenth and twentieth centuries. He lives at Lüneburg.